Henri Stierlin

PHOTOGRAPHS: Anne and Henri Stierlin

ISLAM

EARLY ARCHITECTURE
FROM BAGHDAD TO CORDOBA

TASCHEN

KÖLN LONDON MADRID NEW YORK PARIS TOKYO

Front cover
The minaret of the Great Mosque
of Samarra, Samarra, 848–852
© Photo: Henri Stierlin

Back cover
Cross-section and ground plan of the
Dome of the Rock, Jerusalem, 687–692
© Drawing: Alberto Berengo Gardin

Page 3
Page of a ninth-century Koran with
large, very stylized Kufic script. The
word of the Prophet rules the thought
and architecture of Islam.

Page 5
Carved ivory box, dating from 964,
decorated with peacocks and gazelles
in foliage. From Zamora (Spain), at
the time of the Umayyad dynasty
of Cordoba. (Madrid, Museo Arqueo-
lógico)

About the author and editor:
Henri Stierlin was born in Alexandria
in 1928 and studied Greek and Latin in
Zurich and Lausanne. He subsequently
worked as a journalist and produced
numerous radio and television pro-
grammes on the history of civilization.
He was editor-in-chief of the 16-volume
Architecture Universelle, published by
Éditions de L'Office du Livre. Stierlin,
who has devoted intensive study to
the field of classical architecture, has
already published *Le Monde de la Grèce*,
Paris 1980, and *Grèce d'Asie*, Paris 1986.

© 2002 TASCHEN GmbH
Hohenzollernring 53, D-50672 Köln
www.taschen.com

Edited by Susanne Klinkhamels, Cologne
Design and layout: Marion Hauff, Milan
Cover design: Marion Hauff, Milan; Angelika Muthesius, Cologne
English translation: Editorial Services of New England, Inc., Cambridge (MA)

Printed in Singapore
ISBN 3-8228-1786-4

Contents

INTRODUCTION

The Origins of Islam

The Dome of the Rock in Jerusalem, the Mosque of the Umayyads in Damascus, the Mosque of the Aghlabids in Kairouan, Tunisia, the Great Mosque of the Caliphate of Cordoba, Spain – each of these is a masterpiece of Arabic art, expressing the splendor of early Islam.

The birth of Islam in Arabia in the seventh century A.D. shook the contemporary world. The third great religion of the Book, Islam was based on the preaching of the Prophet Muhammad in Mecca and Medina; and shortly after the Prophet's death, Arab tribes, inspired by the suras of the Koran, began to spread the Muslim faith. Their squadrons attacked the two great empires of Byzantium and Persia, who were fighting over the Middle East.

The Sassanids of Persia and the Byzantine masters of the Christian empire of the East were both overthrown. Their armies collapsed under the force of the camel riders and horsemen who emerged from the deserts of the Arabian peninsula. Within a few decades, the new arrivals had occupied vast territories. A century after the beginning of the Muslim expansion, the caliphs ruled over an empire stretching from Spain to the gates of China. The Sassanid world had disappeared; Byzantium, overwhelmed, had lost many of its Middle Eastern and Mediterranean territories. Islam had brought together, under the green banner of the Prophet, millions of men who had created a new world order.

With the new religion came new practices and rituals requiring special buildings. The structure which Muhammad created in his own house in Medina became the prototype of all mosques. The mosque was a unique place of prayer that met the needs of the Muslim faithful and became a center for a specific kind of gathering. From the end of the seventh century onwards, mosques sprang up – countless variations being conceived in every place and climate. The mosque created spaces never seen before, giving birth to new architectural forms and producing profound innovations in the art of building – as well as giving Islamic civilization an unparalleled vehicle for spreading the faith and collective meditation.

The flowering of this architecture in the Arab world during the first six centuries of the *hegira* – until the end of the Abbasid empire in Baghdad in 1258 – is the subject of this book. It deals only with the buildings which were constructed in the territories where Arabic (the language of the Koran) is spoken. The world of Persia (where Farsi is spoken), the Turkish-speaking regions (in particular, Anatolia) and the principalities of India will not be discussed. Those areas, as well as the Arab monuments built after the middle of the thirteenth century, will be the topic of further studies.

Despite these limitations, *Islam, Early Architecture* covers an immense area, extending from Baghdad to Andalusia, from Syria to Arabia and from Sicily to North Africa. It encompasses the caliphates of the Umayyads of Damascus, later of Cordoba, and of the Abbasids of Baghdad and Samarra, as well as a number of local dynasties – such as the Aghlabids of Kairouan, the Tulunids of Cairo, the Fatimids and Ayyubids, who reigned in Egypt and Syria, the Almoravids and

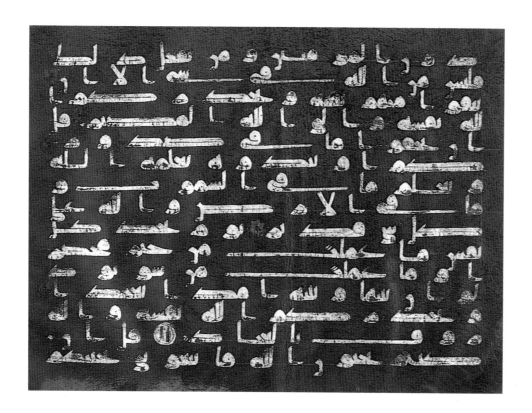

The words of the Prophet
The Koran, the sacred book of Islam which contains Muhammad's teachings, has been the object of special attention by Muslim calligraphers. This page is written in Kufic script on a blue background; it dates from the ninth century A.D. The writing is very stylized and geometric, characteristic of the early centuries of Islam.

Almohads of Morocco and Spain, and so on – apart from areas that came under Islamic influence, such as Palermo under the Normans, or the synagogues of Toledo, which were built in the "Arab style".

Pre-Islamic Origins

The Arab powers did not appear at a wave of the Prophet's magic wand: a long pre-Islamic past in the Arabian peninsula had produced a well-developed culture, now vestigial and still little known. Five or six times larger than France (about 1.2 million square miles, or 3 million square kilometers), but relatively under-populated because of its vast stretches of desert, Arabia is located between the Red Sea and the Persian Gulf, and is bordered by Mesopotamia to the north. It has mountain chains in the south, some of which trap the monsoon winds originating in the Indian Ocean. Thus, parts of Yemen (such as the Hadramaut), and the southern region of Oman (Dhofar) experience rains and are suited to a sedentary existence. Here, agriculture is practised on mountain terraces, and flocks graze on seasonally lush pastures. The valleys are fertile due to the use of dams and irrigation channels. By contrast, date-palms grow only in oases scattered throughout the vast desert areas, encouraging a semi-nomadic life for the tribes who travel in search of pastures for their flocks. The irregular rains of these desert lands provide a rhythm of life which contrasts with that of the farmers of the south, who adapt their environment to their seasonal activities.

There have always been strong tensions between these two groups. But the relative prosperity of the sedentary populations – some of whom occupied fortified villages in the mountains, where they cultivated food crops and gathered the gum of frankincense trees – depended on the mobility of the semi-nomads, for the latter offered the advantage of long-distance trade, by transporting precious spices to the Mediterranean ports.

The populations of the Hijaz, in western Arabia, specialized in trans-desert commerce. Having successfully traded by overland and coastal routes, Arabian seafarers later mastered navigation on the high seas. Taking advantage of the seasonal pattern of the monsoons, they learned to link the ports of Leucecome (on the Red Sea) and Aden to the Malabar coast in India, returning when the prevailing

Founded, tradition has it, by Abraham
The Kaaba, or Black Stone, in Mecca is the heart of the Islamic world, the point towards which all Muslim places of worship are oriented. The *mihrab* in every mosque indicates the direction of the Kaaba towards which the faithful must prostrate themselves. The Kaaba is also the focus of the ritual pilgrimage which every Muslim must make at least once in his lifetime. There he performs ritual circumambulation, a continuation of a pre-Islamic cult.

Arabian landscape
The stretches of sand and graved plains of the Arabian deserts are often bordered by mountain ranges. Throughout these desert territories, a few oases dot the arid expanses with their verdant groves of palms. To protect themselves and their crops from nomadic raiders or hostile tribes, the inhabitants built their mud-brick houses in the style of fortresses.

The mountains of Yemen
In the south of the Arabian peninsula, the mountainous landscape of the Hadramaut region of Yemen receives monsoon rains from the Indian Ocean. Throughout the region fantastic landscapes have been created by man-made terraced fields for growing crops.

winds changed direction. Thus Arabia became an increasingly important trading link between East and West.

The Stages of Development

During its prehistory, Arabia was more temperate and had more rainfall than it does today. But, like the Sahara, it experienced a progressive desiccation which caused its Neolithic populations to migrate towards those areas where the monsoons allowed them to practice agriculture, or towards the oases scattered throughout the desert which offered grazing for their flocks.

Though there have been neither systematic excavations nor sufficiently extensive research to allow reconstruction of the prehistory of the region, Bronze Age burial mounds containing funeral chambers have been found. Arabia was thus in contact with the great civilizations on its borders – Egypt to the north-west and Mesopotamia to the north-east. Documents exist proving that the peoples of the Arabian peninsula spoke a Semitic language related to Akkadian. The earliest references to them by the Egyptians date back to 2100 B.C. and concern commercial links forged to obtain frankincense, a precious commodity which grew only in southern Arabia, and which was necessary for worship rites and for mummification ceremonies. The search for aromatics was the driving force behind these contacts.

In the ninth century B.C., Arabs are mentioned in Assyro-Babylonian texts, in accounts of fighting between Arabian camel riders and Assyrian troops. The princes of Sheba – the Bible speaks of their queen trading with Solomon around 950 B.C. – paid tribute to the sovereigns of Nineveh. In order to conquer Egypt, the Persian King Cambyses allied himself with the Arabs, thereby assuring that his army would be adequately supplied. His Achaemenid successors included Arabia

Yemeni tower houses
Raids and inter-tribal warfare were endemic in southern Arabia – sometimes provoked by the apparent plenty in the southern mountains. Each house was thus built like a fortress.

The art of the Nabataeans
In the early centuries A.D., the small kingdom of Nabataea in north-east Arabia provided lucrative stopovers for spice and silk traders traveling between the Far East and Europe. Its art, schematic at first as seen in this stele, later assumed Hellenistic forms. The Nabataean script, like Arabic and Hebrew, had no vowels.

in their empire, as can be seen on the bas-reliefs of Persepolis (sixth century B.C.). In 539, the satrapy of Arabia was formed. It allowed the kingdom of Arabia some independence, in return for a sizable tribute.

From the sixth to the fourth century B.C., the Arabian principalities of Ma'in, Qataban and Hadramaut were united with Aswan, Himyar, Axum and Yeha on the Ethiopian side of the Red Sea. The construction of three large dams assured Yemen's prosperity. The largest of them, the Marib dam, was almost 2,000 feet (600 meters) long and 50 feet (15 meters) high, made of earth reinforced with stone blocks, each 7 feet (2 meters) long. It was in use until A.D. 575, when the city was destroyed.

In the fifth and fourth centuries B.C., Marib contained great temples made of tall monolithic pillars. The same existed in Auwam and in Almaqa, both contemporary with the Acropolis in Athens. At about that time, Marib had developed bronze sculpture in the round, using the lost wax method. This detached statuary represented figures of the king (or Mukarrib) wearing a lion skin like Heracles, and carrying a dagger similar to those still worn in Yemen. The influence of Greece can be found in the coins, which are copied from the Athenian four-drachma coin.

This civilization, called Himyarite, had its own writing which, like other Semitic scripts, transcribed only the consonants, without any vowels. Its government seems to have been a "parliamentary monarchy" composed of assemblies in which the tribes came together for elections and important decisions.

North of the Arabian peninsula, bordering Palestine, the kingdom of the Nabataeans developed rapidly during the Hellenistic and Roman periods: their city of Petra, in the heart of a mountain range, became a "desert port" which attracted international trade. The influence of late Greek art can be seen in the façades of Petra's great tombs, carved out of red sandstone. All along the incense, spice, and later silk routes, Arabian "dhows" and caravans profited from their geographical position, which gave the region an extraordinary economic and artistic impetus. Between the fourth century B.C. and the first century A.D., the Nabataeans enjoyed alliances in an area of the Middle East where the successors

A thousand years before the *hegira*
The ancient Himyaritic civilization of southern Arabia already had writing with geometrical forms of script. Inscriptions can be found in the Marib, where stone temples and dams bear witness to remarkable development.

of the Diadochi were perpetually at war. In due course, Rome, under Trajan, simply annexed the region in A.D. 106.

During the Roman Empire, Arabia's fortunes fluctuated due to the repercussions of Rome's campaign against the Parthians and later against the Sassanids. Little by little, the route of international commerce shifted from Arabia and the Red Sea to the Persian Gulf and Mesopotamia, crossing the Euphrates near Palmyra, which became the hub of import and export activity. However, once the Parthians (and later the Sassanids) attacked and cut this arterial route, merchants once again took the quieter, if less direct, southern route.

From the first century B.C., a series of more or less independent cities sprang up on the fringes of the great empires: besides Petra, there was Jerash, Palmyra, Dura-Europos and Hatra which were busy centers where a Semitic Arab culture flourished, fuelled by these Aramaean peoples.

The Kingdoms of the Lakhmids and the Ghassanids

This situation prevailed until the Byzantine and Sassanid period, when the creation of "satellite" kingdoms gave some measure of importance to the Arabian tribes bordering the respective empires of Constantinople and Ctesiphon. The Sassanids, with whom the Byzantine emperors were at war, ruled Persia, including

The birth of Muhammad
Orphaned at a young age, Muhammad was raised by his uncle. The cycle of the *Siya-al-Nabi* presented according to the tradition of sixteenth-century Ottoman miniatures, defied the ban on representational images in order to illustrate a "hagiography" of the Prophet. (Topkapi Library, Istanbul)

The family of the Prophet
Muhammad, his face veiled, between his daughter, Fatima, and his son-in-law, Ali, who were his direct descendants. Their heirs thus claimed the legitimate right to govern the Muslim world, causing a split between the Alids and the Abbasids, and creating a schism which divided Shiites and Sunnis. (Topkapi Library, Istanbul)

the area of present-day Iraq; their capital was on the Tigris. They were Zoroastrians and were intensely proselytized by the Nestorian Christians who, being Monophysites, opposed Byzantine orthodoxy.

On the fringes of the two empires, in the area of greatest friction, were two vassal Arabian kingdoms which functioned as buffer states. On the Persian side, there were the Lakhmids, established in Hira, near Kufa, in the middle-Euphrates; and on the Byzantine side were the Ghassanids, occupying the Palmyra region and part of Palestine, with their capital at Basra. But Constantinople's fear of the increasing power of the Ghassanid king at the head of a gathering of Arabian tribes, along with her hatred of Monophysitism, led to the dismantling of the allied forces, whose disappearance was to prove disastrous.

These frontier territories developed close relations with the Arabian tribes and the two great powers which were wearing themselves out in endless wars. Bedouin horsemen became familiar with both the Persian and Byzantine civilizations and their different techniques of warfare. A close relationship existed, before the Prophet Muhammad, between the Arabs and the forces they were later to crush when Islam was proclaimed – indeed, this explains the suddenness of their victory.

The Message of Muhammad

To appreciate the resilience which inspired Arabian Muslim architecture, we must first consider the intentions of Muhammad, and his prophetic work which provided a foundation for the third monotheistic religion to issue from Abraham, "God's friend".

Muhammad was born in A.D. 570 in Mecca, a rich caravan city of the Hijaz, near the Red Sea and the port city of Jidda. He came from a family which had been ruined: he lost his father when he was two years old and his mother at eight. He was raised by his uncle, according to Arab tradition. For many years he led Meccan caravans across the deserts as far as Syria. There he met a Christian monk who seems to have introduced him to the texts of the Gospels. He also made friends with Jews with whom he shared the Semitic heritage of the Pentateuch.

At twenty-five, Muhammad married a rich widow, fifteen years his senior, by whom he had many children, only one of whom survived – a daughter, Fatima. She married Ali, Muhammad's first cousin. Around A.D. 610, when Muhammad was forty, he heard for the first time the Archangel Gabriel speaking to him, imparting the divine call to "Recite the name of Allah" – from which came the name "Koran", meaning "recitation". Thereupon, he began preaching in Mecca and did so for about twelve years. He was generally greeted with scorn by the rich merchants, who refused to believe in the prophetic revelation of someone whose work issued from the writings of the Torah and the New Testament. For in the Koran, Muhammad explicitly mentions Abraham, Ishmael, Adam, Noah, Moses, and Lot, as well as Joseph, Jesus and Mary. He in no way excludes the Christian heritage, any more than that of the Jews.

Faced with the threats of the traders of Mecca, who were alarmed to see him gathering followers, the Prophet decided to leave his native city and go into exile. He emigrated, with a small group of faithful, to the oasis of Yathrib, which from then on took the name of Medinat al-Nabi (the city of the Prophet), or simply Medina. The date of this flight, called the "expatriation", was 622, and it marks the beginning of the *hegira* (*hijra* or emigration), the founding of the Islamic era.

As the head of his little community, Muhammad ruled the oasis, which became the first Muslim "state". As both a political and religious leader, he spent ten years in Medina, studying his revelations which are expressed in highly lyrical language. In so doing, he continued the traditions of pre-Islamic Arabic culture, which had an original literary heritage. In the suras (chapters) of the Koran, Muhammad endowed Arabic with a truly classical polish.

Despite the importance of the mission of its leader, Muhammad's "government" did not neglect daily reality. Muhammad showed his energy and diplomacy in the conduct of his affairs, even organizing the *jihad*, or holy war, with facility – carrying out forays and interrupting caravan traffic going to Mecca, his native city, which he had decided to enter as a conqueror.

His stay in Medina allowed Muhammad to lay the foundations of the religion he proclaimed, and to establish its specific organization. Thus he created the first mosque in his own home. At first, prayers were offered facing in the direction of Jerusalem – thus showing that Muhammad did not wish to break with the symbolic place which, for Jews and Christians, represented the Holy City. The architectural solution which he adopted was inspired by synagogues, in particular that of Dura-Europos, on the Euphrates.

But the break with Judaism occurred in 624, when the representatives of the Diaspora, who were numerous in Hijaz, noted many inconsistencies between the writings of the Torah and the revelations of the Prophet, whom they refused to acknowledge as an envoy of God. The antagonism grew so great that Muhammad expelled the Jews from Medina, going so far as to massacre members of their community. As a consequence, the Prophet decided in 630 that those praying should no longer face towards Jerusalem but towards the shrine of the Kaaba in Mecca.

Similarly Muhammad wanted to include his religion in the continuity of the message of Christ. Since he considered Jesus a prophet on the same level as himself, he did not acknowledge him as the Son of God. He soon met resistance from Christians, and was thus forced to affirm clearly the originality of the path he had chosen.

Six years after the *hegira*, in 628, Muhammad decided to undertake a pilgrimage to Mecca. By a ritual involving walking around the Kaaba, he hoped to put an end to the warlike antagonism which the merchants of Mecca felt towards him. The troops defending the city opposed his entrance. After negotiations, an accord was signed stipulating that the Muslims might make their pilgrimage the next year during a truce. In 629, thus, Muhammad went to Mecca and noted that many people had been won over to his side. A year later, strengthened by the support he could count on, he entered the city in triumph as a military conqueror.

To affirm his message, he broke all the idols in the temple, except for the Black Stone, the Kaaba, which he preserved, for its ancestral cult dated back to Abraham and his son Ishmael, the common ancestor of the Jews and the Arabs. From then on, the Kaaba became the sacred sanctuary toward which all the mosques of Islam would converge. Muhammad subsequently returned to Medina, where, in 632, he died, after having completed his preaching.

With the Koran, the Prophet provided a comprehensive law – divine and human – which included ritual prescriptions concerning prayer and pilgrimage, as well as judicial, cosmological and eschatological provisions. By providing his people with certainty which was to end their inter-tribal antagonism, Muhammad inspired the Arabs and gave them a common aim: to engage in the *jihad*, conceived both as a collective obligation and a way to achieve individual salvation. Thanks to this spiritual impetus, the squadrons charging out of the desert were able to overwhelm the great empires which they conquered in the name of Islam – an Arabic word meaning "submission to God".

Arab Expansion

At the dawn of the seventh century, the situation of Byzantium was not very promising. Heraclius, who ascended the throne in 610, had inherited a disorganized empire. In the 100-year struggle of the emperors against the Sassanid sovereigns, Byzantium had suffered defeat. Syria, Palestine and Jerusalem fell to

Appointed by the Archangel Gabriel
Before the hosts of angels, Muhammad is charged with the duty of "recitation": he brought God's revelation, which his followers wrote down in the Koran. The image of transfiguration conveys the importance of the Prophet's mission. (Topkapi Library, Istanbul)

Khosrau II. The troops of the King of Kings took the holy relic of the True Cross to Ctesiphon. Then the Sassanid conquerors entered Egypt. In 626, Constantinople herself was simultaneously besieged both by the Persians and by the Slavs, allied with the Avars. But Heraclius was an energetic man and he undertook to restock the treasury; he also took the army under his control and restored the unity of the empire. Faced with the success of the Persians, he used a daring strategy and attacked them in Armenia. Thus he forced Khosrau II to evacuate Cappadocia and Pontus. Crossing the Araxes River, he invaded Mesopotamia in 627 and took Ctesiphon. The Persians gave back Syria and Egypt. Heraclius was able to bring the True Cross back to Jerusalem. The next year, in 628, his adversary was assassinated. At a very high cost, the emperor had saved the Eastern Empire. But Byzantium was exhausted. The situation was even worse for the Sassanids. They were beaten and they had lost their old possessions. Persia sank into anarchy – the dramatic result of a relentless onslaught.

For the Arabs, the situation was no better. After Muhammad's death, the apostasy of certain Arab groups ended in fighting. However, these civil wars were quickly resolved, thanks to the fervor which the Prophet's message inspired in the desert squadrons. From 632 to 634, Abu Bakr, one of Muhammad's fathers-in-law (he married nine times, often for purely political reasons) became caliph, that is, head of the Muslim community. Omar, who succeeded him, actually initiated the lightning-swift expansion of Islam throughout the ancient world. He undertook wars of conquest outside the Arabian peninsula. Inspired by a remarkable spirit, the propagators of the Muslim faith quickly conquered Palestine and Syria, snatched from the Byzantine empire after the victory of Ajnadain in 634, and then defeated Heraclius on the Yarmuk in 636. Having no equipment with which to besiege a city, however, the Arab horsemen did not dare attack Jerusalem or Damascus, which were not to fall to them until 638.

The capture of the Holy City represented more than a victory: it was the appropriation of a symbol revered by Jews and Christians alike, which now the Muslims held. For it was on the sacred Dome of the Rock that Abraham had prepared to sacrifice his son when God held back his hand. On this venerable site, the successive temples of Yahweh were erected, the first built by Solomon, destroyed by Nebuchadnezzar in 587 B.C, and then rebuilt once more under the Edict of Cyrus. It was later rebuilt once again by Herod (40–4 B.C.), and finally destroyed by Titus in A.D. 70.

The Temple Mount, called Haram al-Sharif by the Arabs, was also the mythical place of the *miraj*, the point of departure for the "Nocturnal Voyage", whereby Muhammad contemplated the heavens, according to the commentaries of sura XVII, 1, of the Koran: "Glory to Him who made His servant go by night from the Sacred Temple to the farther Temple whose surroundings We have blessed, that We might show Him some of Our signs." The capture of this high ground of the religions of the Book is thus symbolic.

However, the occupation of Syria and Palestine did not absorb all the Arab forces. In 635, some of them had already crossed the Euphrates and launched an assault on the Sassanid empire, then in full decline. They won the battle of Qadisiya in 637, sacked the city of Ctesiphon, and took Nineveh in 641. In the north, they pushed as far as Armenia. In Mesopotamia, the Arabs founded Kufa and Basra, and in 642 they entered the Iranian plateaus after their victory at Nehavend. The whole of Fars fell to them in 644, when their squadrons raided Khurasan.

Their efforts brought the Arab armies simultaneously towards the west. General Amr Ibn al-As invaded Egypt in 640. He founded Fustat (modern-day Cairo) and took Alexandria, which he spared. But a Byzantine counter-offensive forced him to sack the city in 642. Pushing westward, the Islamic forces headed

The death of Muhammad
The Prophet died in 632, with his daughter Fatima by his side. On his death, one of his fathers-in-law, Abu Bakr, became caliph, or leader of the community of believers. (Topkapi Library, Istanbul)

Initiator of the *jihad*
After having retired for several years to Medina with his followers, Muhammad returned to Mecca as a conqueror. From then onwards, the conquests of Islam began to extend across the known world: 100 years after the *hegira*, Muhammad's flight from Mecca to Medina in 622, Arab squadrons had spread the Muslim religion from the Atlantic to the borders of China. (Topkapi Library, Istanbul)

toward Ifriqiya (present-day Tunisia), reaching Tripoli, from which they made raids on the Berbers.

Further east, the cities of Herat and Balkh fell in 654, as well as Seistan. Then the conquerors consolidated their power over Persia and Afghanistan, taking Kabul and Kandahar in 655, after having put Yesdgerd, the last Sassanid ruler, to death near Merv in Turkmenistan.

It took only twenty years to construct this first Arab empire, with Medina as its capital. From 644, the caliph Othman ruled over the destinies of the Islamic world. The territories which he held stretched from Persia and Pakistan to present-day Libya, equalling the greatest of ancient empires. The assassination of Othman in 656 brought a pause in the acquisition of territory, during which the administration of the territories was strengthened and conversion to Islam spread. Ali, the Prophet's cousin, was called to succeed Othman. Infighting between Arab clans destroyed Islamic unity, dividing the Arabs into partisans and adversaries of the new caliph. Muawiya, who had been Muhammad's secretary and then governor of Syria, headed the opposition against Ali. In 660, he was elected caliph, founding the dynasty of the Umayyads, whose capital became Damascus. Having been expelled, Ali fell in front of the mosque in Kufa, under the blows of Kharijite rebels, whose sect would for a long time prove a danger to the caliph's power.

After this bloody interlude, which split the Muslim world in twain, the victorious march continued in 670 with the annexation of Tunisia and the founding of Kairouan. Arab troops then crossed the River Oxus (now called Amu-Darya) in 671, and galloped towards Transoxiana and Khwarizm. Meanwhile, Muslim forces laid siege to Constantinople in 673. They met with resistance from the Byzantine capital, which had mastery of the seas. The siege therefore had to be lifted by the Arabs in 678.

From 680 to 683, the caliph Yazid I reigned in Damascus, during a period marred by the presence of an anti-caliph in Mecca. The Umayyads had to take the city in order to end the secession. At the same time, the son of Ali, al-Husayn, was in turn assassinated in Kerbela in Mesopotamia.

Sixty years had passed since the *hegira*. Where architecture was concerned, it was a period of hesitation. The first mosques were impermanent buildings, whose temporary nature, despite their impressive dimensions, was linked to the events and vagaries of the conquest. The efforts of the Arabs were wholly directed towards military and religious expansion. But the end of the seventh century marked the first blossoming of the arts in the Umayyad empire. This began, with a flourish, in Jerusalem.

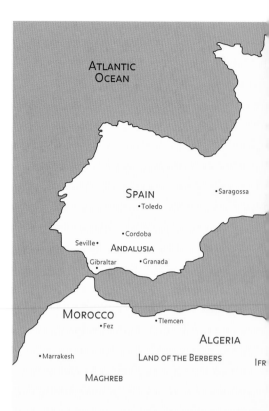

The Islamic West and Middle East
The Muslim world during the early era, showing the principal sites mentioned in the text.

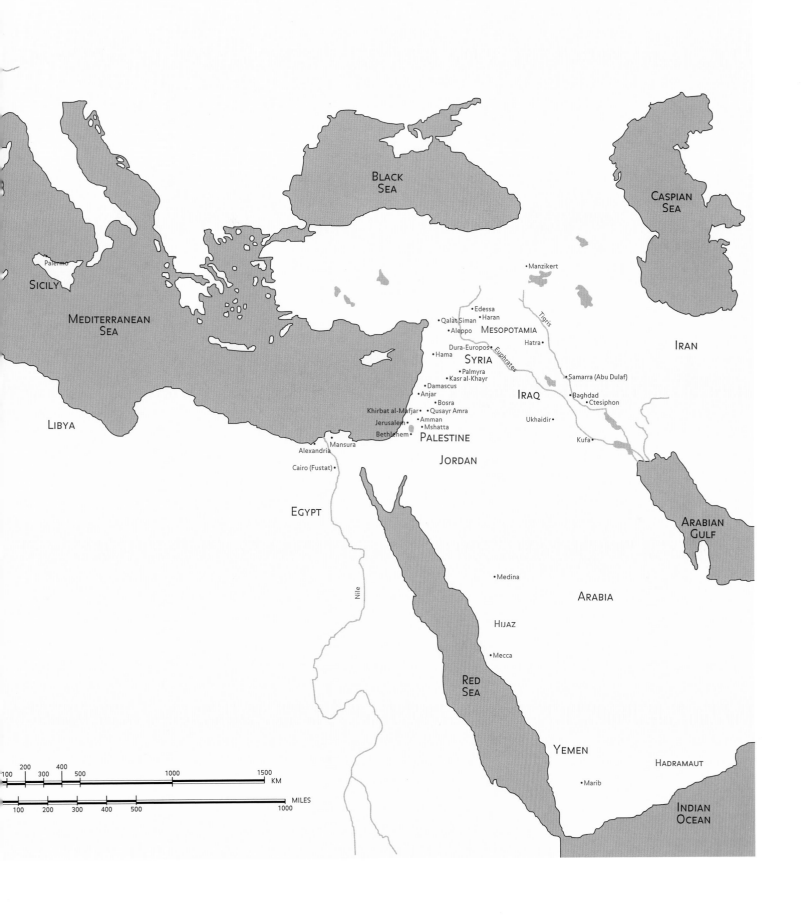

SICILY

Palermo

MEDITERRANEAN
SEA

LIBYA

BLACK
SEA

CASPIAN
SEA

• Manzikert

• Edessa
Qal'at Siman • • Haran
• Aleppo   MESOPOTAMIA
Dura-Europos •   • Hatra
• Hama   SYRIA   Euphrates
        • Palmyra
        • Kasr al-Khayr
• Damascus   IRAQ   Samarra (Abu Dulaf) •
Anjar •   • Baghdad
        • Bosra   • Ctesiphon
Khirbat al-Mafjar • • Qusayr Amra   Ukhaidir •
Jerusalem • • Amman
Bethlehem • • Mshatta
        PALESTINE
                        JORDAN
Mansura •   Kufa •
Alexandria •

Cairo (Fustat) •

EGYPT

Nile

IRAN

Tigris

ARABIAN
GULF

• Medina

ARABIA

HIJAZ

• Mecca

RED
SEA

YEMEN

HADRAMAUT

• Marib

INDIAN
OCEAN

KM
100 200 300 400 500   1000   1500

MILES
100 200 300 400 500   1000

The Dome of the Rock in Jerusalem

عاد قومنك هلاك قلدومسنك دوشمنلرو كى داخى شويله هلاك
قلاءيم دىدى اندن رسول عليه السلام اول برسنى دخى ايلردو

اوفدىدى ايتدى سن بنه موكل سن دى اول فرشته دخى اينك
بن دكز لوصولرا اوستنه موكلم حق تعالى بلوندن انزبغمورز

The First Masterpiece of Islamic Art

Page 21
The *mihrab*, symbol of prayer
The origin and meaning of the niche set in the *qibla* wall of mosques is controversial. This stone *mihrab* with a multifoil arch, dating from the thirteenth century, has a small half-opened door, thus evoking the idea that prayer is the door to heaven. (Archeological Museum, Baghdad)

A new civilization, founded on a new religion, cannot produce artistic and architectural expressions without a cultural heritage from which the forms of an original esthetic develop. The earliest Islamic art flowed from Graeco-Roman thought and creations.

The great sites of ancient Baalbek, Jerash, Tyre and Alexandria still existed for the most part in early Islamic times, having been adapted for Christian use. But besides the inheritance of antiquity, the main source of inspiration in the first decades of Islam came from the accomplishments of the Byzantine world. Indeed, the political organization of provinces, and the state bureaucracy through which the Umayyad caliphs exercised their power, derived from systems put in place by the Byzantine emperors; and the art of Constantinople, just as the continuation of that of ancient Rome revitalized by the Christian empire, had a strong influence on the Arabs.

An Extensive Heritage

A building frenzy took hold of the Christians following the end of their persecution: many edifices appeared in Constantinople and in the eastern Christian empire between the reigns of Constantine and Heraclius (between about 330 and 630). First there were the churches of Constantine and Theodosius, built in the Holy Land – such as the Holy Sepulcher in Jerusalem, the Nativity in Bethlehem, the basilica on the Mount of Olives, and the basilica of St John the Baptist in Damascus. From the fifth century, the Near East was covered with a white blanket of churches, to paraphrase Raoul Glaber.

A new style developed, rigorous and severe and based on the ancient architectural orders, with examples such as the enormous basilica-shrine of Qalat Siman (St Simeon Stylites) and the sanctuary of the pilgrimage of Qalb Lozeh in the north of Syria, as well as the basilica of Djambazde or the shrine at Hierapolis in Anatolia. The sixth century, above all, saw Byzantine architecture reach extraordinary heights in Constantinople. Under Justininan (527–565) wonderful monuments sprang up, the most superb example being St Sophia, with its perfect construction of cupolas and vaults, whose development can be seen in the church in Bosra as well as the cathedral of Edessa.

The central plan of buildings used as shrines was round or octagonal – as in the shrine constructed by Constantine over the cave in Bethlehem, the Anastasis of Jerusalem, the church of St Philip in Hierapolis, or the octagon of Qalat Siman. These formulas, deriving from Roman mausoleums, were continued in Islamic art with the Dome of the Rock and the tombs of the Abbasid era. The Byzantine heritage can also be seen in the outlines and decoration of the buildings: not only are there Corinthian columns (either copies, or examples recovered from older buildings), but there are also mosaics on a gold background, admirably used in Umayyad art in both Jerusalem and Damascus. Finally, palace architecture, baths and small forts, built along the *limes* by the Romans and the Byzantines, influ-

Muhammad's Night Voyage
A brief passage in the Koran suggests that the Prophet went "in spirit" on a voyage which led him to the sacred rock of Jerusalem, the site of Abraham's sacrifice. From there, he ascended into the heavens where, in the presence of angels and archangels, he contemplated Allah. (Topkapi Library, Istanbul)

enced numerous Arab buildings of the first centuries of the *hegira*. This continuity does not arise simply from the perpetuation of forms and techniques, but also because, in the beginning, the Muslims often converted Christian churches, taken from their original owners, into places of worship, before they themselves began building actual mosques. Thus they became familiar with the formal Christian language of architecture, just as Muslim builders in Mesopotamia assimilated the works of the Sassanids.

From Modest Beginnings

The first modest examples of Muslim architecture appeared during the Prophet's lifetime: these were the transformations which Muhammad made to his own home to adapt it to the needs of the faith he was establishing. Certainly, the word "architecture" in this instance is an overstatement, for this was a community where semi-nomads mingled with sedentary Arabs. They used simple shelters, for man and beast, consisting of beaten earth and a canopy of palms. Yet these beginnings provided the fundamental choices which determined classic Arab buildings.

The work of Sauvaget helps us to imagine this first mosque-dwelling erected by Muhammad in Medina. Arab authors describe the Prophet's house as having in the east a series of rooms facing on to a square courtyard measuring around 100 cubits a side (about 50 meters – thus covering around 2,500 square meters), and enclosed by a wall. These vast dimensions stemmed from the camel-drivers' habit of fencing in their herds at night. When it was appropriated for the purposes of prayer by Muhammad's early followers, this courtyard was provided with a lean-to along the north wall. Its roof was made of palm branches and supported by two rows of palm trunks forming a primitive sort of portico. This covered zone offered shade to those who came to hear the words of the Prophet in the *haram* or prayer

The Temple Mount
Between 687 and 692, caliph Abd al-Malik had the Dome of the Rock built on the very spot where the Temple of Jerusalem had stood, in the center of the sacred site on Mount Moriah, the third most holy place of Islam.

Page 25
A sanctuary in the form of a shrine
The Dome of the Rock has an octagonal plan, with a cupola raised on a drum. It is conceived along the lines of a Byzantine funerary rotunda. The original wooden roof was relined with gilded copper, and has recently been restored.

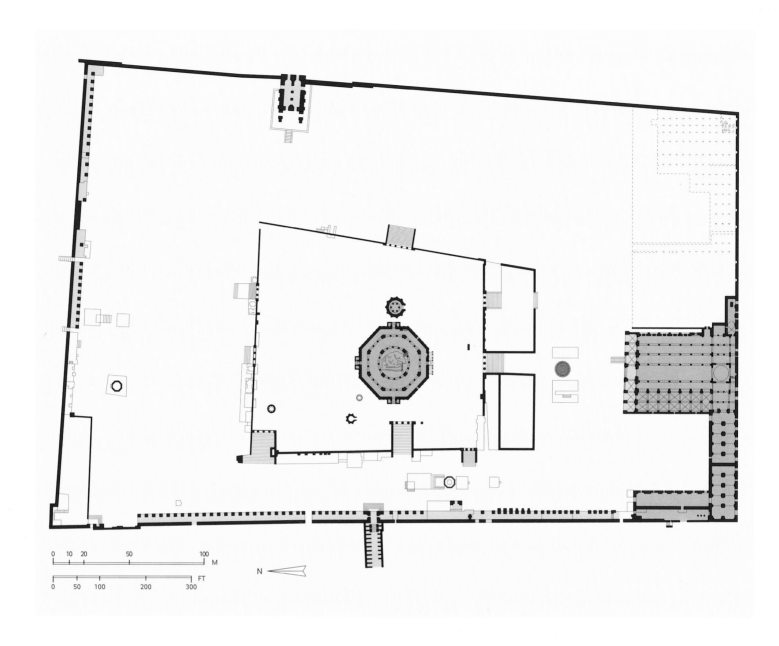

0 0 10 20 50 100 M

0 10 20 50 100 M

0 50 100 200 300 FT

N

hall of this first mosque. This large, rough canopy flanked the wall called the *qibla*, which was perpendicularly oriented towards Jerusalem, marking the direction for prayer. It indicated to the faithful the point towards which they should direct their ritual act of prostration.

Following the break with the Jewish communities of Hijaz, and after Muhammad had entered Mecca, this orientation towards Jerusalem was replaced, in 630, by prostration towards the Kaaba in Mecca (as previously discussed). Since Medina is situated on a line linking Jerusalem to Mecca, the only adaptation needed for the new orientation was the construction of a second portico on the south side of the courtyard, roofed with palm branches. The small Muslim community had grown considerably, so this new portico had three rows of palm-tree trunks acting as columns. Thus the building had a covered structure on the north and south sides. These two palm-roofed porticos were wider than they were deep. The mosque of the Prophet, though rudimentary, nevertheless possessed from the beginning the characteristics of an Islamic space, in contrast to the elongated halls of the Byzantine churches. These hypostyle spaces prefigured the form that the later, great colonnaded mosques of the Umayyad period would assume. Against the wall of the *qibla* there was a sort of wooden seat or pulpit, raised up a few steps, where Muhammad sat to address the faithful. It was the first *minbar,* which was to play an important role in all mosques.

Plan of the Haram al-Sharif in Jerusalem
In the center of the ancient Temple Mount, the octagon of the Dome of the Rock with the al-Aksa mosque to the right, on the same north-south axis. The entire space is considered by Muslims a *haram*, or sacred place of prayer.

Page 27
Magnificent decoration
The blue faïence which adorns the upper part of the Dome of the Rock's façades is an Ottoman addition; but the high marble plinths with geometrical motifs are from the Byzantine tradition of Abd al-Malik's builders.

Indigenous Antecedents

If the characteristics of this first mosque – courtyard, oblong hall, porticos, etc.– were indispensable for early Arab architecture, it was because they corresponded to the spatial concepts of Arab Semitic cultures. What were the archetypes for Muhammad's home in Medina? First, in the pre-Islamic era, a striking example was the temple of Huqqa in southern Arabia, dating from the second century B.C. It had a square courtyard with colonnaded porticos, and an oblong prayer hall.

But there is another even more remarkable "prototype" – the second synagogue of Dura-Europos, dating from the third century A.D. At the end of a small courtyard, flanked on three sides with a portico of stone columns, stands an oblong hall. In the sanctuary is a stone bench, which runs along the base of the walls. The wall at the end of the synagogue of Dura-Europos is similar in plan to the *qibla* of Muhammad's mosque in Medina, with a stonework throne. From the top of the steps, the officiant addressed the faithful in the hall. This throne is a precursor of the *minbar* of the mosque of the Prophet. Furthermore, the synagogue of Dura-Europos has a niche for the holy book of the Torah to the left of the throne. This niche is like the *mihrab* in the mosque. Oddly enough, the first prayer hall of Medina did not contain this fundamental element, which was to be found in all subsequent mosques.

Why was there no *mihrab* in the house of the Prophet? When did this essential architectural element appear in the Islamic world? Such questions are raised by the study of these historical precedents.

The Appearance of the *Mihrab*

The *mihrab* probably first originated from the "prototype" represented by the Torah-niche of the synagogue; though another source was the apse of Christian churches, a form that appeared early in the Coptic chapels of Bawit, in Egypt. The niche, like the apse, derived from the ancient baldachin – a canopy which covered both the statues of the gods and the throne of the deified ruler. It was a symbol of the divine. In the case of the Torah-niche, this construction showed the respect in which the Jews held the Scriptures. For Christians, the symbol of the apse was combined with the triumphal arch (or *ciborium*) over the tabernacle to show the presence of God.

What is the semiological meaning of the *mihrab* for Muslims? Islamic scholars disagree as to the interpretation of this architectural feature. For some (Papadopoulo, Sauvaget, etc.) it is derived from the ancient niche for statues, and represents the "form symbolizing the physical presence of Muhammad in his house". But this interpretation, over-influenced by classical antiquity, seems inappropiate for a Semitic people who condemn the "worship of images", and for whom the ban on all representational sculpture dates back to the Ten Commandments. The *mihrab* of the mosque is not the mark of worship paid to Muhammad, who is in no way equal to God; rather the mosque's function as a place of prayer is to offer a setting for a body of people prostrating themselves before Allah. According to this explanation, the role of the *mihrab* is essentially to indicate the direction for these expressions of veneration. We can thus see in the *mihrab* a symbolic door leading to the hereafter, towards which prayers ascend. Opening on to the divine universe, the bay of the *mihrab* is a concrete representation of man's aspirations to divinity, inviting meditation and leading towards spirituality.

As proof of this interpretation, I offer the example of a small twelfth-century *mihrab* from Mosul (now in the Baghdad Museum) which, in the back of the niche, shows the image of a door, slightly ajar. Such an interpretation is quite different from a desire to "mark the place where the Prophet is to be found". The *mihrab* thus becomes a sign of the absolute, and an affirmation of the divine in this lower

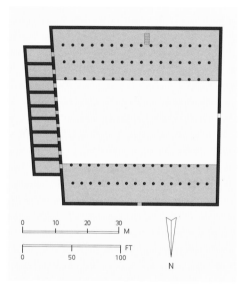

The Prophet's house in Medina
Reconstructed plan of Muhammad's house, converted into a place of prayer, with its porticoes to the north and south bordering a large courtyard. According to Sauvaget, this represents its layout after 630.

world. And since all *mihrabs* face the Kaaba, they all converge towards the same spiritual point, situated in the eternity of God.

Why the first mosque, built by the Prophet in his house in Medina, did not seem to have this niche with its highly spiritual connotations, remains an unanswered question. The change of orientation, first towards Jerusalem and later towards Mecca, may provide some clues.

At the beginning of the eighth century, on the site of Muhammad's house in Medina, the Umayyads erected a vast mosque. They doubled the dimensions of the original building, while preserving its early arrangement of courtyard and porticoes, where the tombs of the Prophet and his two successors were placed. It is with the *qibla* of this venerable hall of prayer that the *mihrab* appeared, "a major innovation of this mosque in Medina", according to Papadopoulo. But this sacred niche in the southern wall of the Umayyad building is new only in the Muslim context. As an architectural symbol, it was (as mentioned earlier) already present in synagogues and Christian churches. Its meaning, associated with notions of veneration and divinity, was merely adapted to the specific content of each of the religions of the Book.

Henceforth, every mosque was to have the same principal parts: a courtyard, an oblong hall, a *qibla*, a *minbar*, and a *mihrab*, implying its orientation towards the Kaaba, to which was added the minaret first used by the Ethiopian Bilal for calling the faithful to prayer. Arab Islamic architecture could then take flight and build its first masterpieces.

From Improvisation to Splendor

Before we consider its major architectural creations, we must emphasize how improvised were the first works of Islam, for the Arabs of the seventh century were not yet builders. The mosques of the campaigns, used by victorious troops and new converts, were rudimentary structures built in the conquered regions. The direction for prostration was often merely indicated by a lance stuck into the ground. Most of these early mosques were simple enclosures with mud floors and walls – or sometimes a ditch in place of a wall, to prevent domestic animals from

The pre-Islamic temple in Huqqa
Plan of an Arab sanctuary from the second century B.C., showing a courtyard with porticoes, a fountain for ablutions and an oblong hall behind a double colonnade forming a vestibule on a raised podium.

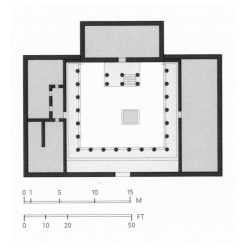

0 1   5   10   15
|__|__|__|__|__|__| M

|_____| FT
0   10   20   50

An architectural precursor
Left: Plan of the second synagogue of Dura-Europos, third century A.D., with its small, porticoed courtyard, oblong hall and niche for the Torah.
Right: "Prototype" of the *mihrab*, the Torah-niche of the Dura-Europos synagogue, with its painted decoration and its two small columns framing the recess which was covered by a semi-dome.

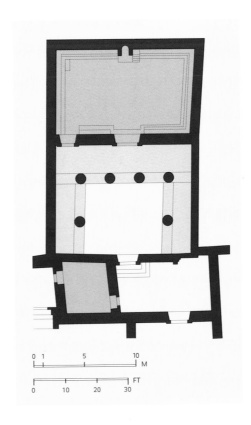

0 1   5   10
|__|____|____| M

|_____| FT
0   10   20   30

fouling the sacred compound. This was certainly true of the first mosque in Kufa, dating from 638, descriptions of which have come down to us through the Arab historians al-Baladhuri (around 892) and al-Tabari (839–923). The colonnaded halls were made of columns and beams taken from ancient monuments such as temples, churches or the buildings of the Ghassanid and Lakhmid emirs.

Despite the rough and temporary look of these mosques erected by the Arab armies, the spread of Islamic buildings was rapid and effective: each town and neighbourhood had its own meeting-place (*al-jami*) where the Muslim community gathered for Friday prayers. There the *imam*, the political, military and religious leader, addressed the crowds from the *minbar*. But in the eyes of the conquered peoples, the rough-hewn aspect of the mosques was often a source of mockery.

Compared to the great buildings of the emperors in Constantinople and the traditional pomp of the Byzantine church, these places of Islamic worship were derided by non-Muslims. Thus Bishop Arculf of Gaul, who visited Jerusalem in 670, less than fifty years after the *hegira*, wrote that the Arabs had built "a crudely constructed building using huge beams laid on ruins" on the Temple Mount. He was speaking of the first mosque to be built on one of the most celebrated sites of Islam – the point of departure of the Prophet's famous "Night Journey".

The Establishment of the Umayyad Dynasty

To blend the cultures of the conquered masses and the conquerors, and to make new converts to Islam, the Arab rulers had to adopt an architectural language inspired by the forms and techniques of the monuments which were the pride of Christianity and the Eastern Empire. But this was not possible until the capital of the Arab world had shifted from Medina to Damascus – a move made in 660 by the Caliph Muawiya, founder of the Umayyad dynasty.

This shift from Arabia, in order to establish the caliph's court in an ancient city of the Near East, was of prime importance for the future of the Islamic world and for its architecture in particular. The choice of Damascus meant that, from the beginning, the Umayyads adopted many Graeco-Roman traditions. The bureaucrats, scholars, mathematicians and officials, who had been brought up in the Byzantine school, became associated with Islamic power from then on. In the world of architecture, where the Arabs did not have a substantial tradition, the Umayyad caliphs put to work Byzantine architects, master builders, sculptors, and mosaicists, or persons trained by them, in order to provide Islam with monuments to rival the principal Christian creations.

In his "Voyages and Grand Tours", the Arab writer Ibn Battuta (who was born in Tangier in 1304 and died in Ronda in 1370) relates that "the Caliph al-Walid sent the Byzantine emperor the following message: 'I would like to rebuild the mosque of our Prophet. Could you help me in this endeavor?' And the emperor sent craftsmen to the caliph." Military and religious antagonism in no way prevented a close collaboration between Christians and Muslims. The mosque at Medina is no longer a good example of this Byzantine contribution to early Islamic art, as it has been burned down and reconstructed several times. Rather, it is the Dome of the Rock in Jerusalem which best illustrates the substantial role of Christian builders in the service of the first caliphs, at the dawn of the Umayyad age.

A Political and Religious Creation

Jerusalem, called by the Arabs al-Quds, was the site of the first masterpiece of Islamic architecture, the Dome of the Rock, famous among all the monuments of the Holy City. With its octagonal rotunda rising above the the Temple Mount, or Haram al-Sharif, it stands on the very site where Solomon, commemorating the sacrifice of Abraham, had the temple of Yahweh built as a resting-place for the Ark of the Covenant.

The Mosque of Medina
Reconstructed plan of the Mosque of Medina, built by Caliph al-Walid between 707 and 709, on the site of the Prophet's house (indicated by the dotted line). Its wide porticoes surround a trapezoidal courtyard. At top left is the tomb of Muhammad and his two heirs (according to Sauvaget).

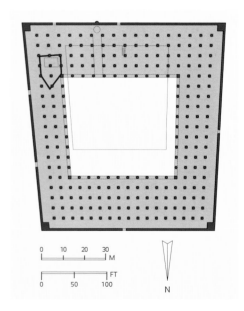

Ritual circumambulation
The double ambulatory of the Dome of the Rock: its octagonal colonnade surrounds a circular portico which supports the cupola. This building, in the form of a Byzantine martyr's shrine, or *martyrium*, is decorated with mosaics on a gold background, and Corinthian columns.

After Caliph Muawiya had decided to establish his capital at Damascus, the tension with Medina continued to grow. This antagonism between Arabia and Syria worsened after the accession to power of Yazid I, thought to have been responsible for the murder of al-Husayn, Ali's son. Immediately, Ibn al-Zubayr, Muhammad's cousin, declared himself caliph at Mecca. This "anti-caliph" remained at the head of Arabia for ten years. The Medina faction expelled the Umayyads from the Holy City. Later, troops from Damascus laid siege to Medina and Mecca to suppress the schism. In 693 the Kaaba was set on fire during the assault, and the anti-caliph was put to death.

Faced with the aftermath of the rebellion of Medina, Caliph Abd al-Malik, who succeeded Yazid I in 685, wished to mitigate the situation in which the faithful found themselves during the insurrection – namely, unable to make their pilgrimages to the holy places of Mecca and Medina. He wanted to divert the flow of Muslim pilgrims towards Jerusalem, an area he controlled closely from Damascus. Knowing that Jerusalem was already a place of pilgrimage for both Christians and Jews, he calculated the financial profit he could make from pilgrims of all three great religions of the Book. In order to attract believers to this highground sanctified by Abraham, he decided to construct a resplendent monument on Mount Moriah. On the site of Solomon's Temple, where Christ had preached and where Muhammad was raised to heaven on his "Night Journey", Abd al-Malik ordered the construction of a building in which the spirituality of Islam would shine forth. He wished to create a masterpiece capable of eclipsing

The cynosure of the Old City of Jerusalem
In the middle of the Temple Mount stands the Dome of the Rock, built in the seventh century, at the center of the sacred site. Its gilded dome shines over the old quarters of the city.

The glittering interior
The magnificent dome dominating the sacred rock of Jerusalem is supported by an arcade with alternating black and white archstones. The arcade is crowned with mosaics, above which are clerestory openings. Precious materials — such as colored marble, gilding and tesserae — lend exceptional luster to the first great religious building of Islam.

the holy places of Arabia, then inaccessible except during rare periods of truce. Furthermore, according to al-Yakubi (died 897), the caliph had forbidden his subjects to go to Medina lest they succumb to the anti-caliph's propaganda. On the chosen site in Jerusalem, the symbolic presence of Abraham was as strong as in Mecca, on the site of the Black Stone of the Kaaba.

The Dome of the Rock was built between 687 and 692. Its design was entrusted to an architect with Byzantine training; the site was under the direction of Syrian master-builders; and mosaicists of Constantinople provided the decoration. This team created a building, in the center of the Temple Mount, which is in the line of the purest tradition of Christian shrines, whose octagonal shape created a central point around which the great ritual circumambulations could take place.

A Geometric Marvel

The Dome of the Rock, or Qubba al-Sakhra, dominates the Temple Mount. Its central octagonal plan is 54 meters in diameter and its cupola rises to a height of 36 meters. The façades of the octagon facing the four cardinal points have doors with porches. The largest, facing south, has a porch supported by eight paired columns, in two rows on either side of the entrance. Dominating the sacred rock, and supported on a drum, is the dome, whose soaring form, suggestive of the horseshoe arch, rises high above.

Inside, there is a double ambulatory used for ritual circumambulation. These ring-like spaces are bounded by concentric porticoes. The outermost is octagonal, and runs parallel to the walls of the building. On each wall of the octagon, there are two columns between the cornerpillars. The portico therefore comprises eight pillars and sixteen columns.

The interior portico is circular, having only four pillars between which there are three columns supporting four arches on either side. Thus there are twelve shafts which, along with the pillars, support sixteen arches surrounding the sacred rock. Above this arcade rises the high, cylindrical drum on which the dome rests.

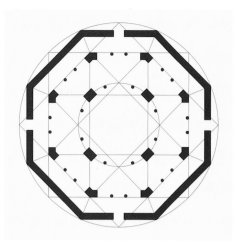

Diagram of the octagon
The geometric layout of the Dome of the Rock is based on the principle of rotating squares, set at 45° angles to one another. The entire building flows from this unifying form, a sort of *mandala* with many numerical implications.

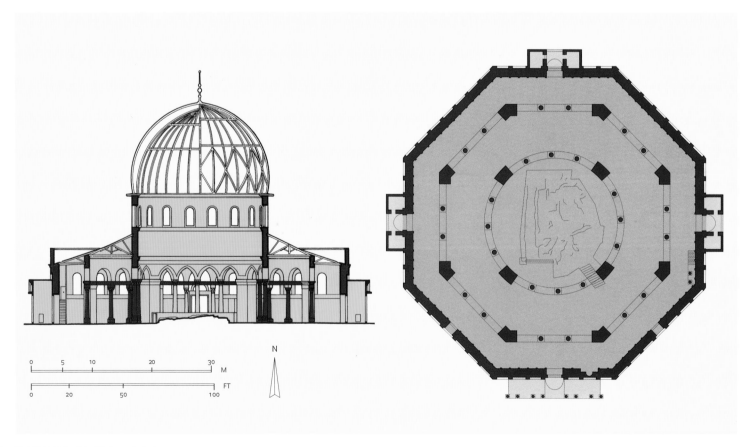

From Abraham's sacrifice to Muhammad's Night Journey
On this rock, surrounded by a portico, the veneration of Abraham and the Prophet converge. Tradition has it that the Prophet rose from here to the heavens mounted on Buraq, leaving the imprint of his foot in the central rock now beneath.

Page 34 below
The perfect central plan
Cross-section and plan of the Dome of the Rock in Jerusalem. The formula of the Byzantine martyr's shrine here reaches its apogee. The cupola rises above the sacred rock, around which is a double ambulatory for ritual circumambulation.

Many authors have studied this remarkable structure made up of circular and octagonal elements, with round and ring-like spaces, and alternating pillars and columns. K. A. C. Creswell and M. Ecochard have analyzed the geometrical forms which are part of the composition of this finely-elaborated central plan. They have noted that the concentric arcades are laid out in the figure of an external circle, with a radius of 26.87 meters or a diameter of 53.74 meters, in which are inscribed two squares set at 45° angles to each other. The intersecting points of these two squares describe an interior circle, with a radius of 20.56 meters or 41.12 meters in diameter, which outlines the octagonal arcade. By connecting together, vertically and horizontally, the eight points of intersection of the two intertwined squares, new intersections are made describing a circle which corres-ponds to the outline of the interior arcade, with a radius of 11.13 meters or a diameter of 22.26 meters. Thus, from the fundamental exterior circle there issue logically two other, smaller circles which describe the entire construction.

Such geometric structures, in which the plan is naturally derived from a single theme, are common in the ancient world as well as in Byzantium. Ecochard has shown that the same composition of an exterior circle with the same diameter is found in the church of St Vitalis in Ravenna (A.D. 540), while the Church of the Ascension in Jerusalem (378) rests on an octagon identical to that of the Dome of the Rock. A similar plan seems to have produced the octagon of Qalat Siman (476), the shrine of St Simeon Stylites in the north of Syria. The Roman-Byzantine conception can be seen in this use of geometry demonstrated by this first great Islamic building.

Ancient and modern authors unanimously praise the spatial harmony, balance and perfection in the Dome of the Rock. Its plan truly reflects ancient mathematical esotericism, corresponding to the Greek philosophers' idea that numbers and simple geometric shapes were a way of comprehending reality. The theories of Plato and Pythagoras postulated that these mathematical concepts were symbols of the ideal, unchanging and perfect world of the hereafter. The microcosm of architecture is thus called upon to translate the laws of the macrocosm. The building helps to express the mystery of the world. This gnostic concept, handed down to Islam by the ancients, opened the doors to a semiology which calls for an in-depth "reading" of architecture.

In the Dome of the Rock, the symbolic is found in the passage from the square to the circle, that is from earth to sky, by the intermediary of the octagon. It is a kind of *mandala*. Through the ritual of circumambulation, the pilgrim experiences the squaring of the circle, the union of body and soul.

On top of the cylindrical drum which emerges from the octagon rises the proud dome, with its gilded copper roofing. This dome was made with two wooden frames, one inside the other. The outer shell, slightly raised and salient, contains an inner shell which is strictly hemispherical. The use of a wooden dome, rather than one of stone, comes from the tradition of the Syrian builders. Indeed, there must have been a wooden frame at Qalat Siman and in the cathedral at Bosra. This solution allows the creation of very light structures which span relatively vast spaces.

Page 36 above

The splendor of the Umayyads
The decoration of the Dome of the Rock in Jerusalem was in the tradition of Byzantine imperial art. Its reused ancient columns, capitals with blossoming corbeils, Byzantine dados and glittering decoration, made the ambulatories of the building a worthy symbol of the rising Umayyad power.

Page 37 above

Marble veneers
The walls of the Dome of the Rock are covered with a veneer of polished marble in geometric patterns – a style inherited from the Roman-Byzantine tradition.

Page 37 below

Place of pilgrimage
The Dome of the Rock was not planned as a mosque, but rather as a place for ritual circumambulation; nevertheless, it has a small, sparsely-decorated *mihrab* to mark the sacred character of the building.

Page 36 below

Multicolored stained glass
The windows of the octagon were probably originally lined with finely-carved marble screens (*claustra*). During the Ottoman restoration, they were filled with sumptuous polychrome stained-glass set in plaster lattice-work, similar to those in the mosques of Istanbul.

The Mosaic Decoration

The sumptuous decoration of the Dome of the Rock is reminiscent of Byzantine ornamental language. The exterior of the octagon was completely redone in the Ottoman period, in polychrome tiles in which the color blue dominates; but the high plinth of marble with geometric motifs, which remains at the base of the walls, is derived from the original veneers and flagstones. Inside, everything expresses Byzantine pomp: the colored marble columns on cube-shaped bases, the gilded Corinthian capitals topped with dados, the outline of the architrave reminiscent of classical antiquity, and above all the sumptuous mosaics, depicting vines and branches on a gold background, which cover the walls and arcades. Everywhere there are floral compositions, with fountains of youth amid an effusion of intertwined leaf-work.

This covering of tesserae evokes the magnificence of the churches of Constantinople or Ravenna. But in the Dome of the Rock there are only plant motifs; there are no human figures. Ibn Battuta, describing this monument, admits to being "unable to find words for such beautiful work".

It is strange that the first architectural masterpiece of the caliphs was not a mosque, but a sort of shrine, a building exalting the rock which was consecrated by Abraham and by the Prophet Muhammad's "Night Journey". The building is not oriented in a specific direction; rather it is the center of a consecrated space, with its four doors corresponding to the four cardinal points. It refers only to itself, and its structure is strictly centripetal. It must be remembered that its creator, Caliph Abd al-Malik, wanted the Dome of the Rock to become the true center of the Islamic world, ousting the pre-eminent position of the Kaaba. Its signal mission was to emphasize the convergence between the three religions which had issued from the Pentateuch.

In this context, the Dome of the Rock cannot fail to recall the first church of the Holy Sepulcher in Jerusalem (335), which is not far from it. There is a deep and purposeful analogy between these two buildings: both have a central plan with a double ambulatory, topped by a cupola with an inner diameter of 20.40 meters in internal diameter; they both house a sacred rock underneath where there is a grotto; in both there is a footprint – of the risen Jesus in the Holy Sepulcher, and of the "messenger of Allah during his ascent to the heavens" in the Dome of the Rock. Such a convergence of form and function cannot be accidental. It is the result of a clear wish on the part of Caliph Abd al-Malik to appropriate the legacy of the Christian religion at the site sanctified by Abraham.

The al-Aksa Mosque

This analogy with the tomb of Christ is not limited to the rotunda alone. For just as the Holy Sepulcher has an addition, beyond an *atrium*, in the form of the Church of the Resurrection laid out on an east-west axis, so the Dome of the Rock received an architectural addition after the insurrection of Arabia had been quelled. This was the al-Aksa Mosque which was built on a north-south axis. It was constructed between 707 and 709 by Caliph al-Walid of Damascus, to replace the jerry-built structure that Arculf had described. This time the Umayyads built a true mosque, orientated towards the Kaaba; it was built in front of the Dome of the Rock, on the side of the Temple Mount. The al-Aksa Mosque has undergone too many upheavals for its original plan to be identified. Only at the crossing – the intersection of the main nave with the bay leading to the *mihrab*, surmounted by a wooden-framed cupola – can vestiges of the original be seen which are sufficiently well-preserved to give some indication of the building's original appearance. There are some beautiful mosaics on a gold background, showing palms and branches, as well as some curious pendentives at the corners, also covered with golden tesserae.

The Jerusalem mosque
Built in 707 by Caliph al-Walid, al-Aksa Mosque stands to the south of the Dome of the Rock with which it forms an inseparable whole — similar to the placement of the Church of the Resurrection and the adjacent Holy Sepulcher. The mosque has been razed several times and rebuilt; all that remains of the original building is the transept above the cupola in front of the *mihrab*.

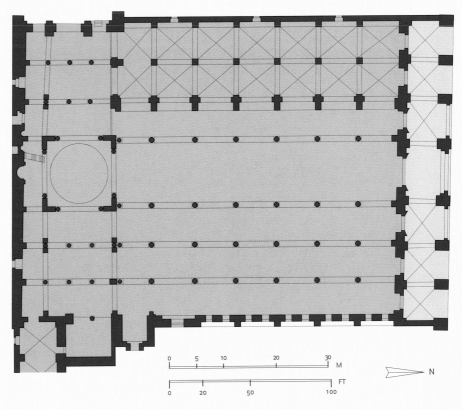

A much-debated plan
Plan of al-Aksa in its present form.
The restoration work on this
Umayyad mosque in Jerusalem
has greatly altered its original
appearance. It seems once to have
had seven naves whose arcades
were perpendicular to the *qibla*.

Nevertheless, the al-Aksa Mosque is a hypostyle with seven naves and arcades which are perpendicular to the *qibla*, and eleven bays which are preceded by a vestibule. The roof must have been entirely wooden, with a flat ceiling. Al-Aksa refers to the covered part of the Umayyad sanctuary of Jerusalem, for the entire Temple Mount (Haram al-Sharif) was considered a vast place of prayer and prostration. This area is none other than the ancient *temenos* of the Temple of Solomon, covering a space of 430 meters by 300 meters, whose central terrace, on which the Dome of the Rock stands, measures 190 meters by 130 meters. The al-Aksa Mosque, adjacent to the edge of the wall, stands on top of ancient Hebrew substructures, called "the stables of Solomon" by Arab authors.

Decorative foliage

The transept, above which the cupola of the al-Aksa Mosque rises, is at the end of the principal nave, bordered by arcades on three levels. Each of the large arches is strengthened by tie-rods linking the imposts, above which are triple bays. Over these, three windows light each bay of the nave. The ceiling is wooden, and the triumphal arch is decorated with mosaic foliage.

Page 41

Glittering pendentives

At the four corners supporting the cupola of the al-Aksa Mosque there is a curious system of pendentives. The transition between the square plan and the circular base of the dome is made using a pendentive, on top of which is a concave circular motif. The entire surface is covered with sumptuous mosaics on a gold background.

The Great Mosque of the Umayyads of Damascus

A Monument in the Image of Paradise

Page 43

The Tree of Life

This detail from a mosaic panel depicts palaces under a tall palm tree. It adorns the treasury of the Great Mosque of the Umayyads in Damascus, illustrating Ibn Battuta's description: "If eternal paradise exists on earth, it is found nowhere else but in Damascus".

The aquatic delights of Damascus

The mosaics adorning the courtyard of the Great Mosque of Al-Walid in Damascus depict marvelous palaces surrounded by running water under eternally green foliage – the image of the paradisal Garden of Eden promised to believers by the suras of the Koran.

"Damascus – may God the Most High protect her – Damascus, Paradise of the Orient, place where His light shines, seal of the land of Islam, young bride whom we have admired, adorned with flowers and fragrant plants: she appears in the green brocade gown of her gardens. On a hill, Damascus is honored to have sheltered the Messiah and his mother – may God bless them – offering them a pleasant refuge, bathed in spring-waters where shade trees spread their freshness and where the stream is like the water that the fountain Salsabil pours forth in Paradise."

This is the invocation with which the traveler Ibn Jubayr (1145–1217) began his description of the capital of the Umayyads. It was in Damascus, at the beginning of the eighth century, that Caliph al-Walid (705–715) constructed a vast mosque worthy of the mighty empire over which he ruled. After laying out the enlargement of the mosque at Medina on the site of the Prophet's house, as well as the al-Aksa Mosque in Jerusalem, to the south of the Dome of the Rock, al-Walid decided in 706 to build a sumptuous place of prayer in the center of Damascus, on the site of an ancient *temenos*. Indeed, the splendor of this Great Mosque of the Umayyads was such that, during the first centuries of the *hegira*, the building was considered the eighth wonder of the world.

The genesis of this masterpiece was complex, mysterious and surprising. But before detailing its phases of development, we must briefly describe the mosque itself – which is 1,300 years old and which, despite having suffered a series of catastrophes (the worst being the great fire of 1893), still has a fascinating beauty.

Situated high on an ancient *temenos* measuring 160 by 100 meters, al-Walid's mosque is orientated east-west, with a rectangular enclosure resembling a fortress. To the north, it has a vast oblong courtyard, 120 meters wide by 150 meters long. The courtyard is surrounded on three sides by arcades and porticoes, the fourth side being the façade of the prayer hall. The *haram* has a central pediment surmounted by a cupola. On each side, there are two wings extending sideways. Each is formed of three bays emphasized by arcades parallel to the *qibla*. This prayer hall occupies the entire southern side of the *temenos*, and measures 136 by 38 meters. The two symmetrical wings extends 56 meters to east and west. Inside, each is divided by two pairs of arcades in the form of porticoes, set on either side of the main central part of the building, which act as a short axial nave. Each arcade is supported by ten massive columns. On top of these shafts, which are linked by large arches, there is a second level formed by bays half as wide, supported by small columns. Thus, above each large arch there are two smaller ones. Such is the structure of the four porticoes which support the roofs of the wings of the mosque.

These load-bearing structures create the prayer space, which faced south. They run east-west, parallel to the southern edge of the *temenos*. At first glance, these are very classical structures, with their columns, Corinthian capitals and arches

topped with dados. The general style is reminiscent of grand Byzantine architecture – like the Dome of the Rock, in Jerusalem. The illusion is so vivid that when entering this great hall with its elongated width, the visitor feels as if it had been turned 90° from its lengthwise axis. Instead of the three bays parallel to the *qibla*, there seem to be three longitudinal naves. This spatial perception is reminiscent of the internal plan of a church. In short, the general structure is misleading, confusing bays with naves, so that the visitor has a tendency to "read" the building perpendicularly, without remembering the actual layout, or the orientation of Muslim prayer towards the Kaaba.

This impression is so strong that more than one scholar has committed the error, in studying the Great Mosque of the Umayyads, of calling the central core of the building a "transept" when, in reality, it is a nave (Creswell), and of calling the bays which divide the wings on either side "naves". For this reason, some archaeologists and historians have suggested that the building is an ancient Byzantine church, simply occupied and remodeled by al-Walid. In order to transform the basilica into a mosque, the caliph, they claim, merely turned the orientation of prayer by 90°; and in the building where Christians had turned towards the east, Muslims turned towards the south, in the direction of Mecca.

This hypothesis was defended successively by Watzinger and Wulzinger, by Drussaud and Diehl, and by Lammens and Strzygowski. But Creswell refuted their theories by showing that a Byzantine basilica would never have had this kind of plan, at the edge instead of in the center of a *temenos*, and that the proportion of a "nave" three-and-a-half times longer than the "transept" would have been incongruous. The truth is more complicated.

The Great Mosque of the Umayyads
A bird's-eye view of the Great Mosque of Damascus, built on the ancient *temenos*, with its minarets and high cupola towering over the old city – where bazaars have replaced the porticoed avenues of the Roman-Byzantine city. The Great Mosque was built between 707 and 714.

The Origins of the Building

The historical origins of the "Byzantine" impression given by the Great Mosque must be identified. In the first century A.D., Damascus contained a celebrated temple dedicated to the Roman God Jupiter. It was at the time of the construction of this Roman sanctuary that the flat, open area – the ancient *temenos* – was built, on which the mosque stands. In the fourth century, after the Christianization of the Empire and Christianity became the official religion, the Temple of Jupiter Damascenus was replaced by a great basilica dedicated to St John the Baptist, during the reign of Theodosius (379-395). Following the Islamic conquest in 635, the *temenos* was divided between Christians and Muslims. According to Arab chroniclers, each group performed its own rites there. It seems that, in the early days of Islam, churches were used often alternately by the two communities.

In about 664, after making Damascus the capital of the Umayyad empire, the Arabs insisted on using the entire area which included the *temenos*. They stopped using the church, next to which they may have erected a first *qibla* of modest dimensions where they placed the *mihrab*, said to be that of the Comrades of the Prophet. Arab authors describing the reign of al-Walid unanimously affirm that the caliph had the basilica of St John the Baptist demolished in order to build his Great Mosque. Such consistent testimony makes it impossible to accept the hypothesis that the Mosque of the Umayyads visible today is the former Church of St John the Baptist modified for Muslim prayer. Furthermore, as Creswell points out, no Byzantine basilica would have had either the proportions or the off-center position this building has. How can these facts be reconciled with the profoundly Byzantine impression created by this prayer hall?

The courtyard portico
The double arcade on the north side of the Great Mosque of Damascus is the result of a medieval restoration which returned to the original arrangement of two levels, and which also replaced the ancient columns – presumably reused elsewhere – with square pillars delimiting the courtyard.

A magnificent space
A view of the north portico and courtyard of the Great Mosque in Damascus with, to the left, the main, central building dominated by a cupola known as the Eagle Dome, which divides the oblong prayer hall into two parts. Al-Walid's building, situated in the ancient *temenos*, inherited imperial Roman dimensions.

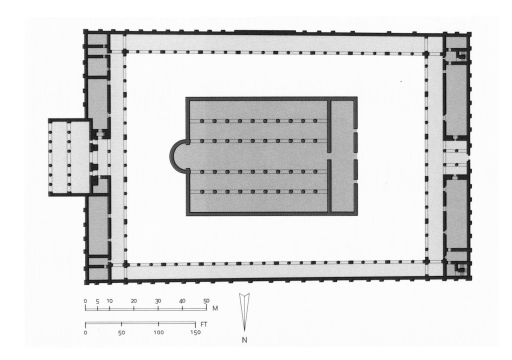

Page 51
Measuring time
The north minaret, which towers over the so-called Gate of Paradise in the Great Mosque of the Umayyads, is the only one built here by the Muslims: the two others rise above square, Christian towers. To the east of the courtyard (on the right) stands a small building which once housed a clock, described in minute detail by Ibn Jubayr who saw it in 1184. He noted that the clock indicated the time of both day and night by using bells and lights.

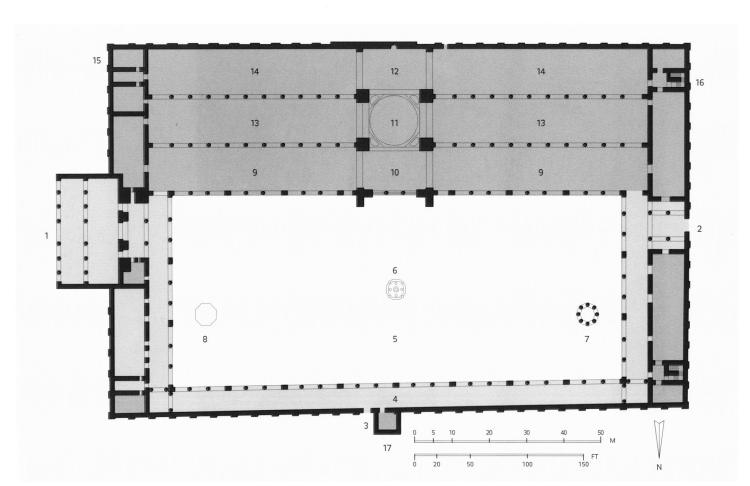

The plan and its controversial origins
Above: The reconstructed plan of the basilica, dedicated to St John the Baptist, dating from the Theodosian era, and built on the ancient *temenos*. This building must have been dismantled at the beginning of the eighth century.

The design of the Great Mosque
Below: The actual plan of the Great Mosque of the Umayyads in Damascus, with its oblong hypostyle hall. The three bays are supported by large arcades parallel to the *qibla*.
1. Original main entrance
2. Western entrance

3. North gate or Gate of Paradise
4. Portico enclosing the courtyard
5. Courtyard on the site of the *temenos*
6. Ablutions pool
7. Small treasury
8. Clock tower
9. Bays of the prayer hall courtyard
10. North bay of the central nave

11. Eagle Dome
12. Central bay in front of the *mihrab*
13. Central bays of the prayer hall
14. Southern bay along the *qibla*
15. Eastern minaret
16. Western minaret
17. Northern minaret

The Contradiction

I propose a hypothesis to settle this contradiction. In order to recreate the origin of the Great Mosque, we must first admit that Caliph al-Walid demolished the Byzantine building and, second, that he built a new building. Furthermore, this building gives the undeniable impression of a church in the Byzantine style.

These suppositions are not contradictory in the light of the common practice of reusing existing materials. Indeed, during the first centuries of Islam architects often reused materials in building their mosques. Examples of this can be found in Kufa, in Cairo at the Amr Mosque, in Kairouan, in Cordoba, etc. – in short, wherever hypostyle halls were built using ancient columns. It was the same in Damascus, but on a much larger scale. I suggest that Caliph al-Walid had the Byzantine church of St John the Baptist demolished with great care. He was especially interested in the great colonnades with their two levels of arcades which he decided to reuse – while changing their position – in order to include them inside the mosque which he wished to erect on the southern side of the *temenos*.

In order to accept this idea, we must imagine the appearance of the Byzantine church that Theodosius constructed on the site of the Temple of Jupiter Damascenus. This basilica most certainly stood in the center of the Roman *temenos*. (Even if this detail has no bearing on my hypothesis, I would point out that the *temenos* had two entrances, the main one to the east and a secondary one to the west. Following the Christian tradition, the basilica, surrounded by a large enclosure, was oriented so that its apse faced east, thus towards the main entrance.) This church, dedicated to Saint John the Baptist, one of the principal contemporaries of Christ, was one of the largest basilicas in the Christian world. It must have had five naves– as did St Peter's in Rome, the Church of the Nativity

The original portico
The gallery on the western side of the courtyard has retained its ancient appearance. The sequence of a pillar for every two columns had delineated the *temenos* of the Roman-Byzantine church of St John the Baptist, only part of which remains.

Page 53
The Treasury
The Treasury chamber, perched on top of eight reused marble columns, is an octagon covered with mosaics on a gold background, and surmounted by a lead-lined cupola.

in Bethlehem and the Church of the Resurrection in Jerusalem. Its proportions of width to length must not have exceeded one to one-and-a-half, following the custom observed for this type of building. The five naves were the result of four large arcades (with two levels of arches) supporting a saddle roof with visible trusses. Conceived in this manner, the building with its apse must have been 65 meters long by 40-45 meters wide (St Peter's in Rome is 65 meters wide).

The four porticoes of the basilica (like the inner porticoes of the mosque today) probably each had ten columns and eleven large arches 4.8 meters wide. Clearly, in the eyes of al-Walid's builders, these forty monolithic columns – more than 6 meters high, with superb Corinthian capitals and keystoned arches, with the second layer of smaller arcades, resting on twenty-one smaller columns – was a valuable construction. Thus they decided to reuse this material.

The caliph's architects proceeded with a methodical and careful dismantling operation, the columns and capitals (which probably came from the Temple of Jupiter Damascenus and had already been reused by the Byzantines!) and the arches being the object of nothing less than an anastylosis ahead of its time. The work consisted of erecting these architectural elements in the southern part of the ancient *temenos* and giving them a new role.

The Eagle Dome

The octagonal cupola of the Great Mosque of the Umayyads was rebuilt after the fire of 1893. Supported on pendentives, the cupola dominates the short central nave, which divides the oblong space of the prayer hall into two equal parts.

The builders of the Great Mosque of Damascus thus merely redistributed this material. In the south of the *temenos*, on either side of the central nave, they placed a pair of arcades parallel to the *qibla*. On top of these structures – where the arcades which had defined the naves of the church would henceforth separate the bays of the mosque – they again used the timber roofing, with the visible trusses of the Byzantines.

It is now easy to see why the Great Mosque in Damascus evokes Byzantine architecture – though it would certainly be difficult to prove archeologically that material was re-used on a large scale. Extensive excavations would have to be undertaken in the courtyard. Besides, it is important to remember that the disastrous fire of 1893 necessitated the reconstruction of a large part of the prayer hall. As for the cupola, according to a tradition solidly confirmed in Syria, it seems originally to have been constructed in wood, as at al-Aksa and the Dome of the Rock in Jerusalem.

Thus, in Damascus, there was demolition and reconstruction. But stress must be laid on the respect with which the caliph's builders dismantled, stone by stone, the old Byzantine church. This care is explained by the fact that this basilica contained a precious relic: the head of John the Baptist. The Prophet Muhammad had mentioned this prophetic character: "While he [Zacharias] prayed standing in the Temple, the angels called him: 'God announces to you the birth of John [Yahya] who will confirm the truth of the Word of God. Great and chaste, he will be a prophet among the just.'" (Koran, III, 39)

The Muslims' veneration of Yahya persists in the Great Mosque of Damascus. In the eastern wing of the *haram* stands a small chapel to which the remains of the saint were transferred. It was logical, therefore, that the church dedicated to this venerable personage, honored in the Koran, should be the object of great attention from the caliph who thus perpetuated, in his own mosque, the memory of Yahya.

The reuse of materials from the sanctuary is not limited to the features of the basilica alone; it also extends to the superb portico around the courtyard. In effect, the *temenos* was surrounded by a gallery of arcades – a gallery which presented a constant rhythm of two columns for one pillar. This portico did not survive in its original form, except to the east and west. In the north, later restorations replaced all the columns by pillars. Like the large arcades of the *haram*, these galleries border the courtyard with a second row of smaller arches. These form pairs of bays, each pair resting on a small column.

The courtyard of the Great Mosque of the Umayyads has in its center a fountain for ablutions, while to the west there is an octagonal chapel supported by eight reused ancient columns. Its upper part, in the form of a monumental casket which was the receptacle for the Treasure, was thus placed under divine protection. The eight sides of this little tower, called Bait al-Mal, are covered with sumptuous mosaics with a gold background. To the east, symmetrically opposite this structure, stands the so-called Clock Tower.

At the two opposite ends of the *qibla*, the mosque is enclosed by minarets which rise from ancient corner towers. A third minaret stands on the north side, on the central axis of the courtyard, thus corresponding to the cupola which dominates the principal *mihrab*. To the right of this northern minaret is the so-called Gate of Paradise.

Sumptuous Mosaics

The notion of paradise, and the evocation of the courtyard encircled by galleries, naturally calls to mind the superb mosaic decoration which once covered the walls of this area, exposed to full daylight. To start with, the entire enclosure of the courtyard was adorned with scenes depicting foliage and rivers, on the banks of which stood dream-like dwellings, nestling beneath shady trees in the cool of an enchanting setting.

Only a small part of this shimmering collection of landscapes, on their gold background, has miraculously survived destruction. The quality of these remnants makes the disappearance of the greater part of such magnificent mosaics all the more lamentable. Originally, a high plinth of marble ran along the galleries and the prayer hall. Around the courtyard, at head height, the marble was faced with fine, multicolored mosaics. The walls and the arcades were entirely covered with mosaics, in which idyllic dwellings by the sides of streams were surrounded by magnificent clusters of leafy plants and clumps of verdant trees. On the façade, the main central structure of the mosque shone forth, including the pediment with its gold vine fronds, and huge multi-storied palatine edifices. Everywhere the Byzantine artists in the service of the caliph had worked to express the comfort and luxury of a better world and brighten this pre-eminent place of worship.

What is the meaning of this exceptional iconographic ensemble in a civilization which rejected figurative images? Certainly neither human figures nor animals are to be found in this natural scenery. But it is reminiscent of the text of Ibn Jubayr, cited at the beginning of this chapter, which evokes the countryside of Damascus,

Architecture of the imagination
The blue-and-gold decorative mosaics of the Mosque of the Umayyads are sometimes stylized, as in this "triumphal arch" inspired by an ancient ideal. The foliage peeping from behind the upper parapet recalls the theme of the verdant greenery of paradise.

at the foot of the Anti-Lebanon Mountains (Jebel esh-Sharqi), whose streams suggested the comparison with the fountain of Salsabil in paradise. Indeed, these mosaics of the Great Mosque of the Umayyads convey an image of paradise, with gardens, trees, rivers spanned by picturesque bridges, villas and pleasure pavilions scattered amidst the cooling shady trees, semicircular palaces and cities reflected in lakes. The mosaicists have conformed to the interdict expressed in the second of the Ten Commandments (Exodus 20: 41), and thus no person appears in this ideal universe.

The representation follows the tiered perspective of ancient art, giving the dwellings a cubist appearance. As for the luxuriant vegetation – which must have seemed miraculous to Muslims from the Arabian deserts – its style foreshadows a kind of pointillism. This mosaic art is in many ways similar to that of the Dome of the Rock and the al-Aksa Mosque, but on a much larger scale and with an infinitely greater freedom of expression.

These landscapes were the work of mosaicists from the ateliers of Byzantium, as Ibn Battuta confirmed: "The emir of the believers, al-Walid [...] asked the sovereign of Constantinople to send him some artisans. He received twelve thousand." They were not all mosaicists, it seems; but the enormous surface of the

Portico on two levels
Elevation of the portico, with its double arcade above, which encloses the courtyard of the Great Mosque of Damascus. The alternating interplay of two columns and one pillar, and the twin bays on the upper level, creates an even rhythm in this surrounding gallery.

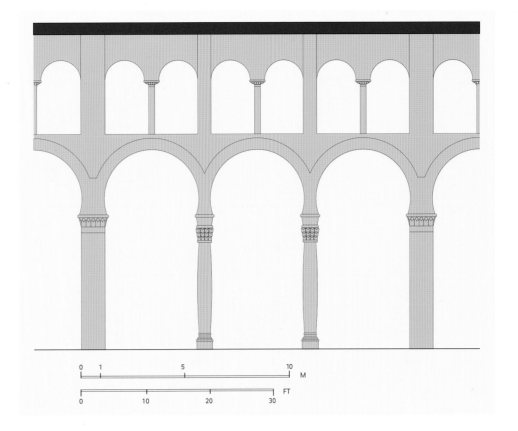

Page 58
The majestic prayer hall
Lateral view of the *haram* of the Great Mosque of Damascus. The ancient, tall monolithic columns, with their Corinthian capitals, and the wide arches with small columns above them, make this hall one of the great successes of early Islamic architecture – despite the prevalence of reused materials.

mosaic-encrusted walls of the Great Mosque of Damascus must have required an army of specialists.

The images adorning the courtyard and the façade of the building stem from a system of symbols based on the description of the joys promised by the Prophet to those who followed the Word of God. And indeed, this divine vision which captivates Islam, precisely translates the terms of Muhammad's message: "God has promised believers, men and women, gardens watered by streams. There they will dwell eternally. He has promised them delicious habitations in the garden of Eden." (Koran, IX, 72). Such descriptions of eternal happiness recur often in the Book: "Here is the garden promised to those who fear God: it is a garden watered by fresh streams. Its fruits are inexhaustible and its trees perpetual. Such is the goal of the believers." (Koran, XIII, 35).

In this consecrated space – once an ancient pagan *temenos*, and later, during the Christian epoch, transformed into an enclosure around a church, like a fortress of faith, a new-walled Jerusalem – the courtyard of the Great Mosque reflected the joys of paradise to come. Paradoxically, though the artists took pains to depict the blessings of the after-life, its torments were nowhere present. In the Great Mosque of Damascus, visitors will look in vain for the tortures to be endured by evil-doers, such as are found on the tympanums of medieval churches. Yet the Koran does not fail to list them. Just as early Christian art shone with revelations and ignored hell, so early Islamic art concentrated on visions of paradise.

Linking Past and Future

With this Great Mosque of Damascus – whose splendor provided an antechamber to paradise, harbinger of the future bliss promised by the Prophet – Caliph al-Walid created a work capable of competing with the greatest Christian sanctuaries. The Commander of the Believers exalted the memory of Yahya, the herald of Christ, safeguarded the Byzantine heritage of the old Theodosian basilica of St John the Baptist, reusing massive elements from the old structure in his mosque, and employed teams of mosaicists from Constantinople to illustrate the radiant future for believers. Thus he was not only respecting the spiritual and material legacy of the past, he was also creating the first imperial mosque, the proud model which was to inspire numerous Islamic creations in the following centuries. He had, in fact, created the dazzling model of the Muslim prayer hall.

On either side of the short nave, surmounted high above by the cupola, called the Eagle Dome, which covered the area in front of the *mihrab*, were two great wings which flanked the *qibla*. This arrangement permitted al-Walid to create, between 707 and 714, the grandiose prototype of Islamic space, a wide place where, in order to pray, believers kneeled side-by-side, without any hierarchical arrangement, in contrast to the lengthwise naves of churches and basilicas, where the faithful are grouped behind each other based on a strict order of precedence.

These two conceptions of space – one elongated and widthwise and the other lengthwise, in several successive rows – demonstrate the differences between two specific perceptions: that of the inhabitants of the desert, horsemen who rode side-by-side in a single row across a wide expanse, and that of the residents of fertile land criss-crossed by roads, on which groups and bands traveled single-file. Between these two concepts lies a fundamental contradiction; they are separated by a different understanding of the nature of space.

In imposing its conception of space through the way in which the faithful place themselves during prayer, the Muslim religion thus affirms an original approach to the spatial environment which is conveyed in the layout of the mosque. In this respect, the work of al-Walid in Damascus is a model which influenced all the great hypostyle creations, such as the mosques of Amr (in Cairo), Kairouan, and Cordoba, not to mention the mosques of the Abbasids in Samarra.

Let us not forget that this oblong space issued from the layout which, at the outset, had been a shed made of palm-tree trunks with a covering of palm branches built by the Prophet himself at his home in Medina. By adopting this oblong configuration, the hall of the Great Mosque of the Umayyads of Damascus merely established a formula which reproduced in monumental fashion the venerable model which Muhammad had bequeathed to his followers.

Thus Islamic prayer (deliberately or otherwise) expressed a perception of the world which came from the immense desert spaces of Arabia, homeland of the Prophet. And less than a century after the *hegira*, the meeting place of believers embodies this concept by giving it a magnificent material form. Never before had architecture so fully expressed the innermost mentality of a people, and the reflection of their faith.

The holy of holies
Beneath the central cupola of the Great Mosque of Damascus, the principal *mihrab* and the *minbar* form the most sacred space in the building. Both are the outcome of a restoration project following the 1893 fire.

Umayyad Palaces

Agricultural Estates in the Deserts of Syria and Palestine

Page 63
Builders at work
A rare mural of the Umayyad period shows workers on a building site hauling quarry blocks. From the decoration of the audience hall of the small palace of Qusayr Amra, in the Jordanian desert, dating from the beginning of the seventh century.

Ancient heritage
Detail from a decorative frieze in the Umayyad palace of Mshatta, which was unfinished when the dynasty came to an abrupt end in 750. The decoration of palmettes and acanthus leaves is a direct descendant of the style of late antiquity.

The palaces discovered in the Syrian desert were long thought to be hunting lodges where nostalgic Arab princes tried to recreate the ancestral experiences of gazelle-hunting expeditions in Arabia's vast deserts. These buildings, dating from the Umayyad period, are often of a remarkable quality and highly ornamented. They combine the luxury of public baths with the pomp of banqueting halls, apparently springing from the imagination of a leisured aristocracy. In the past few decades, they have been the object of intensive studies which have changed our understanding of them. Jacques Sauvaget and Oleg Grabar have shown that these buildings – sometimes fortified – were not palaces designed for the sole pleasure of the prince, but rather centers of vast farming operations which belonged to the caliph or to Arab chieftains.

These buildings were on the frontiers of the Roman, and later Byzantine empires, in the heart of the fertile crescent between Palestine and the river-basin of the Tigris and the Euphrates, and in the Bekaa Valley. The region has always been fought over because of its potential richness, for it is blessed with regular rainfall. However, agricultural activity was difficult to maintain in these regions when the Parthians and Romans, and later the Sassanids and Byzantines were at war with each other.

The plains between Lebanon and the Anti-Lebanon also had regular rainfall, while areas of Jordan and Syria, which also had good arable land, needed to be irrigated. But the development of irrigation systems requires long-lasting political stability, and thus it was not until the "Arab Peace" of the seventh and eighth centuries that these areas once again enjoyed the prosperity they had known in ancient times, at the height of Palmyra's prosperity. With an ambitious construction scheme, including dams, reservoirs, canals, aqueducts, wells, water-wheels, water catchments and even sometimes drainage pipes, the Arabs developed productive agriculture. This took the form of plantations, and amounted to the creation of oases in the desert. These new landowners reclaimed the land between the wheatfields of the valleys and the deserts. There were at least ten agricultural centers, remains of which have been unearthed by archeologists; while aerial photography has revealed enclosures built to protect the fields and orchards from herds of nomadic animals.

Farmers in the areas surrounding the irrigated plains of Jazirah (between the Euphrates and the Tigris) had the best water supply. Extensive single-crop cultivation became intensive, with rice paddies, and plantations of sugar cane and cotton. But in these alluvial areas fewer buildings have survived since they were usually made of sun-dried brick.

By revealing the important agricultural function of these princely desert domains of the Umayyad era, archeologists have allowed us a better understanding of their role. Armed with these discoveries, specialists have often dismissed the function of the pleasure pavilions which were attached to such desert castles. Today we are more even-handed in admitting that one type of building does not necessarily preclude the other. It could be that, at these productive "farms", the Arab aristocracy organized hunting parties, since these areas bordered the desert.

Indeed, these palaces may have had other roles than agriculture and hunting – they were equipped for official receptions and courtly ritual, with all its magnificence. For the Arab court had inherited from Rome and Byzantium not only their bureaucracy, revenue collectors and official administrators based in Damascus, but also their protocol and their liturgy, their pomp and their particular customs. And wherever a prince stayed, he was accompanied by impressive ceremony.

The Country Palaces of the Umayyads

The Umayyads constructed numerous buildings in the vast territories where the caliphs and the members of the Arab aristocracy lived. For their nomadic habits were such that the caliph did not remain in Damascus all the time. Depending on the seasons, his whims and obligations, he liked frequent changes of residence. The same was true for the tribal chieftains who followed the caliph, and adapted

their country houses for their trips away from the capital. This practice would explain the many buildings, traces of which have been uncovered by archeologists in the thinly-populated and today semi-arid wilderness of Syria and Mesopotamia. The best examples, both near Palmyra, are the Umayyad castles of Kasr al-Hayr West and the two compounds of Kasr al-Hayr East, one of which covers 5.4 acres (2.2 hectares).

The desert palaces have very different forms. Most are reminiscent of the Roman or Byzantine forts which bordered the ancient *limes* on the frontiers. These have buildings with a square plan, with round towers at the corners and in the curtain walls. A fortified portal, on the main axis, opens on to a central courtyard, around which are the living-quarters, the mosque, the state reception room and the baths. This strictly rectangular and sober plan can vary greatly in its dimensions – from a small fort with sides of 40 meters (Kasr Kharana), up to castles with sides of 130 meters (Mshatta) and even a small 400-by-320-meters city (Anjar). The square plan is not always followed, either because of additions, which could double the area of the palace as at Khirbat al-Mafjar, or simply because the formula of the Roman camp was not appropriate. Such was the case when an asymmetrical plan was preferred for small public baths, which linked a courtroom with bathing facilities, on the model of the ancient baths (as at Qusayr Amra).

Furthermore, there was great variation in the methods of construction and dec-

Palace or fortress?
Though not threatened by any apparent danger – isolated in the arid desert near Amman – the hunting lodge of Kasr Kharana, with its austere silhouette, is reminiscent of the small Byzantine forts which guarded against Sassanid assaults.

A small boundary fort
The small Umayyad palace of Kasr Kharana, near Amman, resembles the forts which first the Romans, and later the Byzantines, established on the eastern *limes*, or fortified boundary of the empire. Its square plan, with corner towers and a gate in the center of the southern rampart, makes it an example of the *castrum*, or military camp (from which the word "Kasr" or "Qasr" derives).

Plan on a grid
Square plan of Kasr Kharana showing its central courtyard commanding a series of peripheral rooms near the boundary wall.

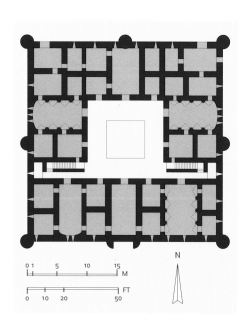

oration. This was an eclectic architecture in search of its own identity. Sometimes builders used Byzantine masonry, alternating layers of stone and brick, at other times they preferred the handsome magnificence of ashlar faced with baked brick. There are external façades covered with a thick, rough-rendered surface, while the rooms have stucco walls; elsewhere, walls are decorated with sumptuous stone sculptures, with scrolls and vines, like Byzantine capitals and friezes. Also in Byzantine style were the extraordinary floors of geometric and figurative mosaics which covered the rooms of the baths; while the painting was unquestionably of Christian origin, with figures and hunting scenes sometimes adorning the ceilings of the throne room. The sculptures adorning the baths and the large stucco statuary are either of Sassanid origin or copied from ancient models. The source of these ornamental motifs is either Near Eastern Christian or Persian.

To illustrate the variety of forms and their inspiration, it is worth studying some of these "desert palaces" on the Syrian and Jordanian borders, as well as those in the Jordan valley and on the banks of the Euphrates.

Small Castles: Kasr Kharana and Qusayr Amra

Built not far from Amman on the fringes of the Jordanian desert, Kasr Kharana resembles a Roman *castrum*. Its square plan, its high walls pierced by loopholes, punctuated by round towers and built of alternating layers of rubble and brick, as well as its high, fortified gate, all give it the appearance of a Roman or Byzantine frontier fort. This castle was constructed around 710, under Caliph al-Walid. On either side of the entrance there are stables and vaulted guard houses. Around a square courtyard, bordered by a portico, there is an axial hall surrounded by

A utilitarian design
The small courtyard of Kasr Kharana, with its surrounding double level of rooms, is not burdened with needless ornament. Both the materials and techniques are very sober. On the ground floor are stables and a guardroom; while above, vaulted apartments form the building's essential elements.

Original vaulting
Kasr Kharana is a surprising mixture of Byzantine and Sassanid influences, as seen in the crossed ribs supporting the roof (opposite) or the great masonry arches resting on clusters of imbedded columns (below).

rooms, whose symmetrical arrangement is repeated on the second level; this is reached by two staircases, one at the east and the other at the west side of the building.

The architectural interest of the building lies in the halls, where barrel vaults have transverse arches supported by groups of three small, embedded columns. This type of roofing recalls the Sassanid style, while the stucco is reminiscent of Persian constructions. This building, adjacent to cultivated land, showed no signs of having been permanently lived in, according to Oleg Grabar, nor was it in use for very long.

Qusayr Amra is a different matter. Here we have a curious public-bath type of building, whose vaults and cupolas are reminiscent of the Baths of the Hunters at Leptis Magna, which date from the end of the Antonines. The building's asymmetric shape rose above the desert wilderness, on the edge of the Butum Wadi, which today is practically dry, but where clumps of oleander reveal the presence of subterranean water. This water source must once have been collected to irrigate the surrounding crops and to supply water for the prince's baths.

Qusayr Amra had a square audience chamber with three parallel, barrel-vaulted naves supporting two large, longitudinal arches, with a 6 meter span. The central nave led to an alcove in the form of a small throne room, where the ruler must have appeared in all his majesty. It was flanked on the right and left by rooms, with apses in the form of semi-domes (called culs-de-four), probably used for ceremonial purposes. All these rooms formed the building's apse-like extremity. The internal space of this throne room – which is no more than 24 square meters – was completely covered with very unusual paintings. The "frescoes" depicted hunting scenes, nude women bathers frolicking under trees, and several people clothed in ceremonial robes – all unusual subjects in the context of an Islamic building. They were treated in a late Hellenistic style, and showed four sovereigns who seemed

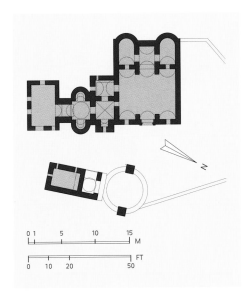

Baths in the desert
Plan of the bathhouse built by an Umayyad prince at the beginning of the eighth century in the Jordanian desert. The building has the usual sequence of rooms found in ancient private baths, as well as a large reception hall. Below, the outbuildings.

to be rendering homage to the proprietor of the palace, in this case the caliph. Indeed, these full-length portraits are recognizable as kings of this era: on one side, Caesar (Emperor of Byzantium) and Roderick, the last Visigoth King of Spain; and on the other side, Khosrau II, King of Kings of Persia, and Negus, King of Abyssinia. Inscriptions in both Greek and Arabic identify these figures and allow us to date the castle of Qusayr Amra in the reign of al-Walid, soon after 711.

This sumptuous throne room was flanked to the east by small bathrooms, and in particular, a strange space acting as a *caldarium*, or Roman hot bathroom, with a hemispherical cupola covered with astronomical and astrological paintings. The Arabs had always been interested in the art of divination and the horoscope: their leaders were obsessed with seeking answers to questions about the future. Thus an enormous emphasis was placed on knowledge of celestial mechanics. This explains why the Arabs made notable progress in astronomy and techniques of observation, developing to a remarkable degree the science they inherited from the Greeks, in particular Claudius Ptolemy.

Great Palaces: Mshatta and Khirbat al-Mafjar

The great Umayyad palace of Mshatta, also situated near Amman, uses the plan of the square Roman and Byzantine fortifications – but on a much larger scale than Kasr Kharana. Mshatta's surrounding wall, punctuated by twenty-five semicircular towers and a false parapet walk (all defensive devices now purposeless) enclose very interesting structures, even though they were unfinished in 750, at the time of the downfall of the Umayyads.

This castle was evidently designed for ceremonial purposes which, shortly after its construction, were no longer required. The square space, with sides of 130 meters (forming an area of 4.2 acres), was divided north to south into three sections, the central one reserved exclusively for the caliph. Behind a central

Nymphs rising from the waves
It is somewhat unexpected to find nude maidens depicted on the murals of the Qusayr Amra reception hall. The proscription of images applied only to religious works at that time.

A miniature *aula regia*
Qusayr Amra has only one large hall, the roof of which consists of three parallel barrel vaults resting on two large, longitudinal arches. The hall has a central apse where the sovereign sat enthroned. All the internal surfaces are covered with paintings, some of which have suffered from the ravages of both time and man.

Bathing beneath the stars
One of Qusayr Amra's bathing rooms has a cupola which bears an image of the sky and the signs of the zodiac. Astrology played a prominent role in the court of the caliphs – consultations of horoscopes were associated with the exercise of power.

entrance, flanked by the mosque on the east, a first room, with vaults running lengthwise, led to a second oblong space 23 meters deep which, in turn, opened on to a vast square courtyard with sides of 57 meters. At the far end of this court-yard rose the palace buildings themselves.

Like the castle itself, the section reserved for the caliph was divided into three parts. In the center was an area with three naves, separated by two porticoes, leading to a triple apse in the Byzantine style. In fact, a room with three exedras, typical of the chevet, or apse and ambulatory of churches in fifth-century Coptic architecture, came from similar formulas handed down from late antiquity, like, for example, the Piazza Armerina palace in Sicily.

This central core of the building is framed on either side by symmetrical apart-ments, whose trefoil-shaped spaces, ending in apses, are vaulted with semicircu-lar arches of baked brick. The load-bearing members – pillars or columns – are made of courses of large, cut stones. The capitals and the friezes along the entrance gate reveal a very elaborate technique of leaf work and interlaced vines, which seem more like art of late antiquity than Arabic art. As with the mosques, the decoration of secular architecture seems to be directly descended from Roman and Byzantine techniques.

The triple apse of Mshatta is reminiscent of the Great Palace of Constantin-ople. Here, ceremonies took place which must have borrowed a great deal from Byzantine customs; they culminated in the appearance of the sovereign, majest-ically attired, as servants parted the curtains held closed while the family and ambassadors prostrated themselves before him.

The great palace at Khirbat al-Mafjar, near the rich oasis of Jericho, is perhaps the most original accomplishment and the most interesting handed down to us by the Umayyad civil architects. The building was divided into three parts, the oldest

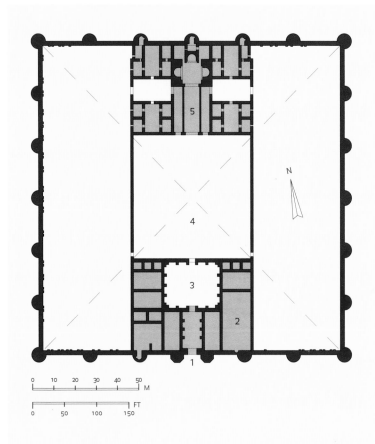

General view of Mshatta
In the middle of a huge square (each side measuring 130 meters) stand the ruins of the unfinished palace of Mshatta, including the remains of its *aula regia* (throne room), which has a triple apse in the center, in the style of a Byzantine courtyard.

In the style of a Roman camp
Plan of the Umayyad palace of Mshatta. The palace has twenty-five towers set in a symbolic defensive wall – for no parapet walk runs around it – and uses Roman vocabulary to create an impression of imperial pomp. Behind a monumental entrance (1), with a mosque to the right (2), the ceremonial courtyard (3) leads to a square covered area (4) after which comes the palace building itself. In the middle, the *aula regia* adopts the plan of a church (5).

of which, the actual castle, was in the shape of a 44-meter square. Like Kasr Kharana, it had round towers at the corners and a central courtyard with porticoes. To the north was an esplanade bordered by a mosque. Behind the mosque was a building which is today almost completely destroyed, but which must have been impressive. Covering an area 30 meters square and buttressed by three semicircular exedras on each side, this audience chamber was raised on sixteen pillars (four rows of four each), forming five naves and five bays. These powerful cruciform supporting structures, divided by small corner columns, stood on a sumptuous mosaic floor covered in geometric designs with no fewer than thirty-one different designs of Graeco-Roman inspiration.

This hypostyle hall must have been completely vaulted. It had thermal installations to the north, with warm and hot rooms, a steam room with a hypocaust, and a small private room where a mosaic has been uncovered with the most remarkable animal figures of early Islamic art. This sumptuous creation was used as the audience chamber, where the Umayyads held their official ceremonies, whose form was inherited from Hellenistic and Roman models by way of the Byzantine world.

Finally, on the eastern side of the palace of Khirbat al-Mafjar, there was an open area 130 meters long, in the center of which stood a fountain. Here was erected a system of arcades and waterspouts within a 12 meter square, containing an octagon, and another central square inside that. This configuration was highly symbolic, demonstrating the power of the sovereign over water, expressed by the supply from an advanced hydraulic technique.

Stone accompanying brick
Mshatta, which dates from the end of the Umayyad period, uses elaborate architectural techniques which contrast with the simpler solutions of Kasr Kharana and Qusayr Amra. Vaults and apses are constructed with remarkable care, incorporating pilasters and columns, capitals and friezes in the antique style. To the right, the western apse of the triple apse is made of baked brick.

Page 77 above
Finely-chiseled stone
A plinth, adorned with delicate foliage and arabesques, in the Umayyad palace of Mshatta. The sculptors imitated ancient techniques and motifs, while demonstrating a *horror vacui* (aversion to empty spaces) which became a leitmotif of Islamic art.

A Princely City: Anjar

Anjar, in the Bekaa Valley, is not so much a castle as a small, rectangular city measuring 320 by 400 meters, which in many ways reproduced the plan of a Roman foundation such as Trajan's Timgad or an imperial palace such as Spalato (modern Split), built by Diocletian. Built by al-Walid between 714 and 715, this city was situated on a fertile agricultural plain. It had a quadrangular outer wall with forty round towers. Orientated north-south, it was divided by a *cardo*, like its Roman models, and by a *decumanus*, formed by wide colonnaded avenues intersecting under a tetrapylon, with four columned portals. Here, the Graeco-Roman tradition

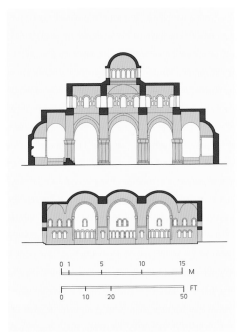

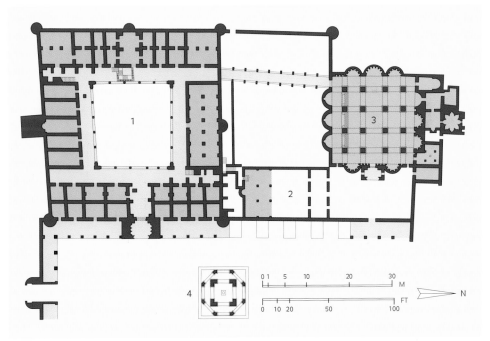

The palace of Khirbat al-Mafjar
Left: A restored section of the vast hall of Khirbat al-Mafjar near Jericho helps us understand a building which today is almost completely razed.

Right: General plan of Khirbat al-Mafjar:
1. Square "castle" with courtyard
2. Mosque
3. Hypostyle bathing hall
4. Fountain shrine

In the rich Bekaa Valley
The lofty porticoes of the Umayyad city of Anjar in Lebanon: Reused Roman columns and capitals decorate this small city where Arab princes withdrew during the hot summers. The complex, built by al-Walid, is contemporary with the Great Mosque of Damascus.

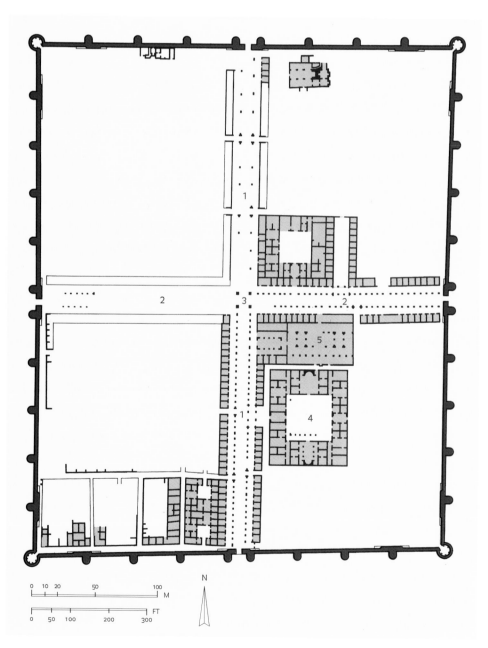

The intersection of the *cardo* and the *decumanus*
Plan of Anjar, based on a Roman design, with its two large avenues, the *cardo* (1) and the *decumanus* (2), lined with porticoes and intersecting at right-angles beneath a tetrapylon (3). In the south-east corner is a palace with a courtyard (4), on each side of which are halls with apses. The mosque is to the north of the palace (5).

Page 79
The elegance of Anjar
The builders of Anjar used ancient architectural features – curved marble columns, Corinthian capitals and corbeils – and the Byzantine method of alternating layers of dressed stone with layers of brick.

was mixed with Byzantine modes of construction – layers of brick alternating with courses of masonry. Some ancient Corinthian columns were taken from Baalbek and reused to support the arcades surmounted by dados, adopting the methods used by the master-builders of Constantinople. In the south-east quadrant of Anjar rose the caliph's palace. It was built round an open rectangular area surrounded by porticoes; it had two basilical halls facing each other, whose apses marked north and south, allowing the specific development of imperial rituals. Behind the palace was the mosque – an oblong prayer hall supported by columns.

The richness of Anjar, which can be seen in its arcaded streets and its palace buildings, depended on intensive agricultural production, made possible by the presence of water for irrigation. Single crops of grain, and later sugar and cotton (which replaced flax), assured the city considerable revenue.

The Urban Palace: the Kasr Amman

The Umayyad sovereigns were not sedentary: they felt confined in the palace in the capital. Thus, besides the country residences discussed above, they also built regal homes in several cities of their empire. No trace remains of the palace which must have stood to the south of the Great Mosque of the Umayyads in Damascus – but in the city of Amman (ancient Rabbat Ammon, later Philadelphia) are remains of a remarkable throne room, dating from the Umayyad era. Crowning the citadel, in the very middle of the acropolis, stands the Kasr Amman which, with its cruciform structure, is an interesting example of Arab palace architecture. Its square hall bordered by four *iwans* (vaulted, rectangular rooms with one open side),

A little-known building
For a long time Kasr Amman was ignored by scholars. Its square structure with masonry vaults, on the site of the ancient city of Philadelphia, is an Arab palace of the Umayyad era.

Design with patterns

Detail of the pattern of arabesques, palmettes and rosettes adorning the blind arcades with imbedded columns at Kasr Amman, which dates from the Umayyad period. Here, reminiscences of antiquity have produced a simplified design language.

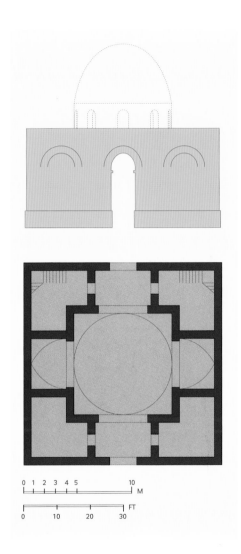

Cruciform palace

The central plan of Kasr Amman, with its double symmetry of four *iwans*, shows Sassanid influence. It must have had a wooden cupola over the center of the structure, where the throne room was located.

shows the influence of Sassanid Persia. Long considered a work of the Ghassanid princes, this edifice built entirely of dressed stone must actually have been a throne room built in the Umayyad era. Its crossing was possibly covered with a wooden cupola on a drum – in the Syrian and Byzantine manner; but the absence of archeological research on this building leaves many unanswered questions about details of its construction.

The vaults of the *iwans* with their slightly pointed arches, and the decoration of unpolished leaf work adorning the blind arcades of this building, suggest oriental influence – perhaps that of Persia, which alone can explain the originality of this work, long ignored by archeologists. In the Umayyad period, oriental borrowings were limited, compared with stylistic devices borrowed from Syria, Palestine and Constantinople and seen in both religious and secular buildings.

Rustic decoration
Arches in the throne room of the
Kasr Amman, whose triangular
archstones show a preference
for the more basic elements of
Sassanid Persia over Roman-
Byzantine forms.

Umayyad architecture fed on the Roman and Byzantine past – and it also anticipated the far-reaching developments, founded on the Persian heritage, which
were to be accomplished by the Abassids. But the western influence was not lost.
The site of Ukhaidir, south of Baghdad, shows the resurgence, at the end of the
eighth century, of the fortified castle in quadrilateral form, with surrounding walls
and defensive towers and an organization dictated by a rigorously rectangular system. On the other hand, Samarra was soon to witness the large scale flowering of
the cruciform plan of the *iwans*, of Sassanid origin. For in Mesopotamia, architecture took on more majestic and grandiose dimensions than those of Damascus –
though they were also more impermanent.

Page 83
The beautiful central area of the
aula regia
The throne room at Kasr Amman.
The lack of thorough excavations
makes it impossible to do more
than conjecture about the
form and material of the roofing
that covered this square area with
its four *iwans*. The most plausible
hypothesis is that it was a wooden
cupola – like that of the Dome of
the Rock.

The End of the Umayyad Dynasty

The Umayyad dynasty lasted less than a century (660–750) and gave early Islam
remarkable architectural masterpieces. Under the reigns of the caliphs Abd al-
Malik and al-Walid, great Muslim architecture flourished. During this period, the
Roman and Byzantine influence dominated. But soon unrest and disturbances
affecting the eastern part of the empire foreshadowed upheavals, and a gradual
shift east of the center of gravity of Islamic power. The last Umayyad caliph,
Marwan II (744–750), moved his residence to Haran, in Upper Mesopotamia, to be
nearer the center of the revolts which broke out in north-east Iran. In 747, the
Umayyad garrisons of Merv and Herat were driven out of these cities where the
uprisings spread fast. Finally, in 750 the caliph was defeated and fled to Egypt. He
was assassinated along with the rest of the Umayyad family. Only one member
escaped. He founded the emirate of Cordoba, soon transformed into a caliphate,
in Spain, at the westernmost extremity of the empire. There, the genius of the
high Islamic culture of Damascus continued for another 250 years.

Umayyad Splendor in Cordoba

An Arab Civilization in Spain

Page 85

A bronze from Umayyad Spain
This deer from the Umayyad palace of Madinat al-Zahra, dating from the second half of the tenth century, confirms the Islamic tolerance of images – even of three-dimensional statuary – during the time of the Cordoba caliphate. This detail shows the stylization of such figurative pieces. (Archeological Museum, Cordoba)

When the family of the Caliph Marwan II was massacred in 750, a single member escaped. This was Abd al-Rahman, who fled to North Africa. The Umayyad caliphs of Damascus had reigned for ninety years over the Arab empire. By 750, the Islamic world extended from the Atlantic to the gates of China. But the upheavals caused by the assassination of Marwan and the accession of the Abbasids in Mesopotamia allowed the fugitive not only to save his life but also to carve out a kingdom in Spain, at the other end of the Mediterranean, where the splendor of Umayyad civilization was re-established.

Abd al-Rahman contacted his relatives and allies who lived in al-Andalus (Andalusia or "Vandalusia" – the Iberian peninsula – whose name derives from the Vandal invasions). A number of supporters rallied to him, uniting under his banner. Thus he took Seville, then entered Cordoba following a victory that allowed him take the title of emir in 755. When he came to the throne, Abd al-Rahman made Spain the first secessionist region of the Islamic empire, at a time when the Iberian peninsula had belonged to the Muslims for less than fifty years.

Victory over the Visigoths

It was in 711 that the horsemen of Islam had gained a lightning victory over the kingdom of the Visigoths. Christian Spain collapsed, almost without resistance, in the face of the troops led by Tariq. At the head of 12,000 Berbers from North Africa, Tariq crossed the Strait of Gibraltar, originally with the mere intention of carrying out a raid on the rich Spanish lands. But the weakness of the Visigoth resistance caused Tariq to transform a looting foray into a permanent occupation. A century after the Prophet had begun preaching in Mecca, Islamic conquests were still just as swift and unexpected. How could a century-old, unified kingdom succumb to an army of a few thousand warriors bent on plunder? The victory can only be explained by the formidable impetus of the new faith, which had already given the Arabs and their allies half the ancient world. Furthermore, the Muslims benefited from favorable circumstances here, too. At the end of the seventh century, the Iberian peninsula, which had been subject to "coups d'etat", sank into chaos. Soon civil war tore apart the Visigoth nation, divided between the followers of Roderick and those of Akhila. The latter took refuge in Ceuta, on the African shore of the Strait of Gibraltar. There the ruler of the city advised him to enroll Muslim forces to fight against Roderick, who had just acceded to the throne of Toledo in 710. Thus it was a Visigoth Christian who summoned the Islamic troops, counting on them to help him carry out his designs on the throne.

Another factor may have played an important role in the Muslim conquest: the Jews were being persecuted in Spain and had prayed for an end to the monarchy in Toledo. They were in contact with their fellow Jews in North Africa, who encouraged the Arab Berber troops to embark. Thus Tariq, ruler of Tangiers and lieutenant to the Arab Musa ibn Nusayr, crossed the Strait and landed in the province of Cadiz. Roderick – who was in the north of the country suppressing a Basque

The art of ivory sculpture
Continuing a late-Roman tradition, sumptuously decorated ivories were characteristic of the splendor of palace life. This medallion on the so-called casket of Leyre comes from Cordoba, and dates from the end of the tenth century. It depicts a bearded king, identified by an inscription as Abd al-Malik, framed by two servants, one holding a fly-whisk and the other a fan and a flask.

revolt – returned in haste to the south. He gathered together a powerful army and attacked Tariq. Considering that the time had come to switch to Akhila's side, some of the Christian troops defected. The Muslim victory was complete. After this success, Tariq decided to keep moving. He subdued Cordoba and continued on towards Toledo, the Visigoth capital, which surrendered. He claimed Astorga, the center of Asturias, and Lugo, in Galicia, before turning towards Segovia, finally re-entering Toledo victorious in 712.

Meanwhile, Musa had brought in 18,000 Arabs as relief troops. He conquered Merida and took the major cities of the peninsula. By 714, all of Spain was under Muslim domination. The Arabs called it al-Andalus. Islam was to remain there for almost eight centuries.

The Work of Abd al-Rahman

When the Arab Berbers were setting themselves up on the Iberian peninsula, rivalry developed and deepened between Tariq and Musa. Both had disobeyed Caliph al-Walid's orders, so he called them to Damascus to account for their actions. From 714 onwards, Musa had to entrust the government of Spain to his son, Abd al-Aziz, who pacified the country before being assassinated on the orders of Caliph Suleiman (715–717).

With the arrival of Abd al-Rahman, who took over the reins of power in 755, Spain became an independent emirate. But the throne of the last of the Umayyads of Damascus was still threatened, and the sovereign needed recourse to bloody repression to foil several attempted "coups-d'etat" fomented by his fellow Arabs. He had to deal with Charlemagne's expedition against Saragossa and his devastation of Pamplona. But this operation, which brought the future Christian emperor

The Great Mosque of Cordoba
A view from the top of the minaret of the prayer hall of the Great Mosque of Cordoba, built from 785 to 961, with its arcades covered with saddle roofs perpendicular to the *qibla*. Above and to the left is the Renaissance cathedral, built in the Mosque's *haram*.

to the borders of Spain, was finally settled in 778 by the defeat of the Franks at Roncesvalles, at the hands of the Basque insurgents who were always ready to rebel.

During the thirty-three years of his reign, Abd al-Rahman made Cordoba his capital. In 785, he laid the plans for the Great Mosque which became (two centuries later and with several enlargements) one of the masterpieces of classic Muslim architecture. In its first version, this 70-meter square building (covering about 5,000 square meters) consisted of an oblong hall (following the Islamic tradition) preceded by a courtyard, also wider than long. The hypostyle hall had eleven naves with arcades perpendicular to the *qibla*. The space is divided into twelve bays resting on 110 columns, recycled either from Visigoth or more ancient buildings. As in Damascus, the reuse of building materials helped to dictate the construction of this mosque, in which marble columns and capitals were retrieved from the ruins of ancient cities ravaged during the great invasions. The façade of the courtyard, supported by massive pillars, was largely open to the bays, allowing light into the prayer hall, which was covered with a timber roof.

A row of doors
Western façade of the Great Mosque of Cordoba: with each enlargement, new doorways were built leading into the prayer hall. Erected by the Umayyads in their capital on the north bank of the Guadalquivir, the Mosque has bays topped with merlons, which lend it a defensive appearance.

In the reigns of Hisham I (788–796) and later al-Hakam I (796–822), the Mosque of Cordoba was not modified. It was not until the arrival of the emir Abd al-Rahman II (822–852) that the first enlargement brought the number of columns in the hypostyle hall to 200. At the time of that construction, from 832 to 848, the area doubled, the *qibla* having been moved south-west, for the building had to be oriented towards the Kaaba. But the number of naves had not changed.

Eighty years later, Abd al-Rahman III (912–961), who proclaimed himself caliph in 929, undertook a second round of enlargements. He enlarged the hall towards the south-east, and placed a square minaret, 34 meters high, at the edge of the courtyard. A few years later, al-Hakam II (961–976) made further modifications, giving the monument its final appearance. The prayer hall was transformed from an oblong area into one running lengthwise, still 70 meters wide, but was 115 meters long, with 320 columns.

These thirty-two bays and the *mihrab*, in the form of an octagonal room preceded by three cupolas with intersecting ribbed vaults, which in turn was bordered by multifoil arcades, gave the Great Mosque at Cordoba its original character. We will return to those elements peculiar to the Umayyad style in Spain. But we must first consider a final and extensive enlargement of the prayer hall, undertaken in 987, at the time of al-Mansur, grand *cadi* (Palace Master) of Caliph al-Hakam II, and later all-powerful minister of Hisham II. Until 987, the building had developed by

continually moving the *qibla* back towards the south-east, in order to keep the symmetrical plan. This time, however, eight naves were added to the length of the prayer hall to its left (towards the north-east), making a total of 224 additional columns. From then on, the mosque at Cordoba contained 544 interior columns and forty-four interior pillars. There were thus 606 supports. The interior area measured 130 meters in width and 115 meters in depth, thus re-establishing the original oblong appearance, following the Islamic spatial tradition.

A large interior space, such as formed the *haram*, requires proportional height. However, the ancient and Visigoth columns gathered by the Muslim architects from all over Spain – and from as far as Provence – were not as tall as those reused in the Great Mosque in Damascus. In order to make up for this drawback, the architects had recourse to an original formula, which was the great innovation of the Cordoba hypostyle, using a system of two superimposed arcades, supporting the flat roof by a series of longitudinal, parallel barrel vaults.

In these complex load-bearing members – inspired by the Roman aqueducts in Merida and Segovia – the upper arch was semicircular, while the lower one was slightly horseshoe-shaped. This solution produced a series of lofty arcades. The capitals, like the columns, were generally old – though copies were often used in extensions made by al-Hakam II and especially by al-Mansur. The load-bearing members were raised by piers which supported the upper arcade. The arches were composed of alternating red and white stones, a Byzantine motif which gave a visual sense of great lightness to this whole system of two-tiered supports. The alternation of light and dark materials was called *ablaq* decoration in Arabic.

The Hypostyle Space

The Great Mosque at Cordoba, the largest place of prayer in all western Islam, demonstrated the potential of a hypostyle space. With its 600 columns covering a multitude of naves and bays over an area of 3.7 acres (1.5 hectares), the building extrapolated by multiplication and repetition all of the previous solutions. Before the unfortunate addition of the Renaissance cathedral, a visitor entering the hall must have been awed by this profusion of columns and arches: in every direction there were receding vistas which vanished in the half-light and seemed to create an atmosphere of endlessness. This character largely survives today, despite the presence of the Christian building in the center of the mosque.

All the elements of the hypostyle mosque at Cordoba combined to make it one of the most original creations of Islamic civilization, from the horizontal space, whose invisible limits accentuate its immensity, to the forest of columns and the constant lightness of the superimposed arches, whose bicolor arch stones seem to vibrate with the light. Never before had such a vast interior space been conceived, using such simple methods as columns supporting arches of limited dimensions. Neither the hypostyle halls of the Egyptian temples in Karnak, Luxor and Edfu, nor Roman basilicas (such as the Basilica Ulpia), nor the churches of Constantinople were comparable. Never had space been so light and transparent. Large Roman cisterns such as the Piscina Mirabile of Misenum or the Byzantine tank at Yerabatan Saray in Constantinople, may have given rise to comparable formulas: but because of their function, these can in no way be compared to the mosques of the Muslim world.

With the Cordoba mosque, Islamic architecture had reached the apex of a system which had previously been illustrated by the Amr Mosque in Fustat (present-day Cairo) or the Great Mosque of the Aghlabids in Kairouan. And the hypostyle space was to be used many times in the Maghreb, under the influence of Muslim Spain.

Unending designs
The geometrical imagination of Muslim artists is expressed in the rhythmic interlacing of a variety of decorative systems. The marble tracery screens in front of the bays of the Great Mosque of Cordoba, are carved with seemingly unending designs.

Sumptuous Decoration

The decoration of the Great Mosque of Cordoba was the work of Caliph al-Hakam II, especially in the area of the *mihrab* and of the *maqsura* which surrounded it. In many respects, the decoration of this prayer hall carried on the traditions of Jerusalem and Damascus; a continuity can be seen in the Umayyad style. However, it is important to remember that 150 years separate the two Near Eastern creations and the Andalusian one in its final state.

The *maqsura* at Cordoba is architecturally very fine. *Maqsura* is the Arabic term for an enclosure surrounding the principal *mihrab*, delimiting an area destined for the sovereign. This formula – which runs counter to the original egalitarian ideal of Islam – is linked in certain architectural aspects to the iconostasis of the contem-

The 600-column space

The vastness of Cordoba's hypostyle hall shows clearly in this
axonometric view which gives
some idea of the original
appearance of one of the caliph's
marvels, before it was disfigured
by the Renaissance cathedral
built in the reign of Charles V.
Among this forest of shafts,
the believer was able to find a
uniquely Islamic space.

The casket of Hisham II

This masterpiece, dating from 976
and part of the treasury of Gerona
cathedral, is made of gilded
and nielloed silver on a wooden
base and is decorated with pearl-
studded palmettes. The border is
inscribed in large Kufic script,
wishing the Emir of the Believers
the benediction of Allah.

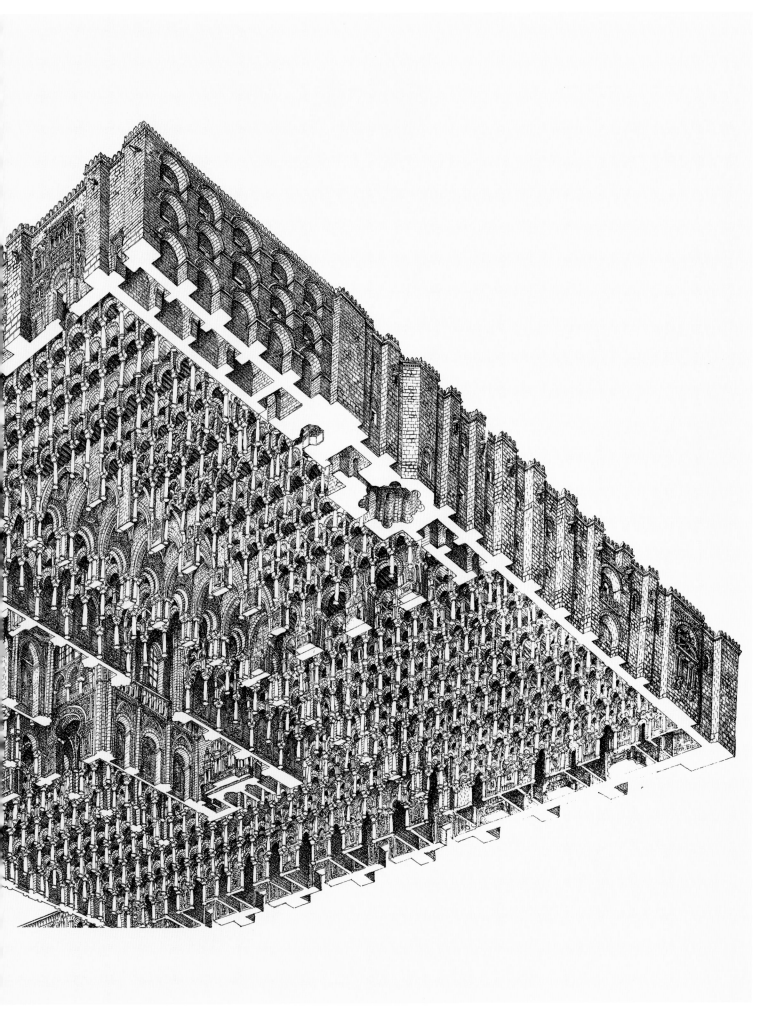

A labyrinthine system
Under a frame of roof trusses, conceiled by a sumptuous ceiling accentuated with painted and gilded motifs (above), are super-imposed arches, supported by a multitude of mostly reused marble columns, that create a lofty and mysterious space in the prayer hall of the Great Mosque of Cordoba.

An ingenious supporting structure
Elevation of three bays of the double-level arcades of Cordoba's Great Mosque. These superimposed arches may have been inspired by the Roman aqueduct of Merida.

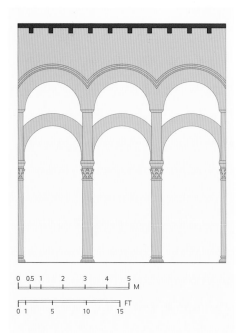

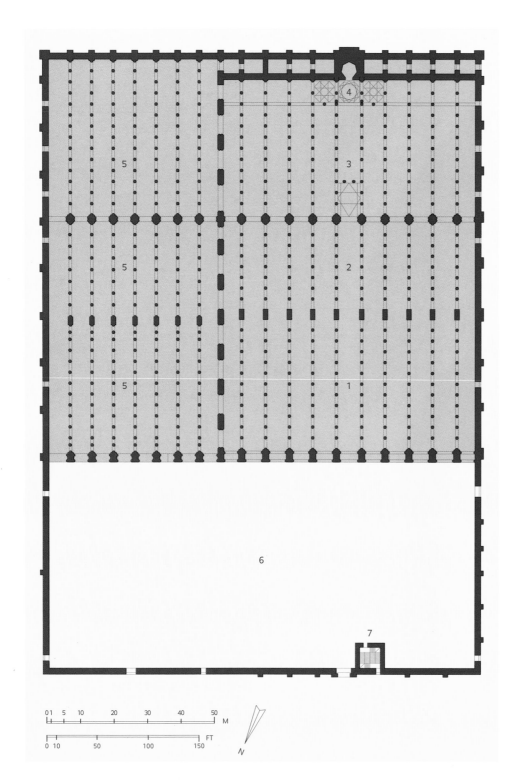

The last stage of the successive enlargements of the prayer hall, made between 785 and 987: here early Islamic architecture in the western part of the empire reached its apogee. The building covered 3.7 acres and had 19 naves with porticoes on columns set perpendicular to the *qibla*.

1. The prayer hall in 785
2. The enlargement of 832
3. The additions of 929
4. The *maqsura* and the *mihrab* covered with mosaics created in 961
5. The enlargement of 987
6. The great courtyard
7. The minaret

porary Mozarabic churches of northern Spain, in which the holy of holies was hidden. At Cordoba, the *maqsura* is bounded over an area equivalent to three naves by intersecting multifoil arches of an exceptional richness. This play of arcades crossing each other creates the effect of a *claustrum*, or pierced screen, which enhances the sacred place of the mosque.

The sumptous decoration of the prayer hall, emphasizes the *mihrab*. The niche takes the form of a small octagonal room – indeed, instead of a simple recess in the *qibla*, Cordoba has an enclosed space, covered with a small cupola in the form of a shell, supported by six multifoil arches held up by small columns.

The astonishing configuration of this *mihrab* is a focus of attention. It is no longer a simple niche but a space entered through a large horseshoe arch, forming a proper "door". The *mihrab* was in no way a "niche for statues": rather, it was a

Refined structures

Above: Schematic drawing of the interlaced arches of the *maqsura* marking the area reserved for the caliph in front of the *mihrab*. Under semicircular arches, multifoil arches encompass sometimes one and sometimes two intercolumniations.

Page 99: Cross-section of a cupola showing intersecting ribs above a secondary *mihrab* in the Cordoba Mosque, after an engraving by Girault de Prangey (1841).

means of access to the hereafter. It was plunged in darkness and filled with impenetrable mystery which suggested the infinity of God.

This formula was frequently to be used again in Andalusia and in the Maghreb – for instance, in the oratory of the Aljaferiya Palace in Saragossa, the Great Mosque of Tlemcen, the Qarawiyin Mosque in Fez, the Friday Mosque of Tinmal, the Great Mosque of Seville, etc. This space was even darker because it lay behind the flamboyant and sumptuous horseshoe arch, covered with polychrome mosaics and gold tesserae. The decoration of the large arch stones around the *mihrab* arch consists of abstract fruit and flower forms on an alternately gold, blue and red background. Around this arch was a kind of square architrave, in relief, called the *alfiz*, which characterizes Islamic architectural language. These frames are also covered with mosaics, on which a quotation from the Koran is transcribed in two lines of Kufic script, in gold on a blue background. (The Arabic writing called Kufic – from Kufa – is usually reserved for the Holy Book. It is recognizable by its angular stylization, sometimes square and sometimes with long upstrokes, which gives it a monumental solemnity.)

The spandrels – the area between the arch of the *mihrab* and the frame of the *alfiz* – are adorned with marble sculptures of large, stylized palm trees. This carved marble is found both in decorative bands alternating with mosaic friezes and in large panels, which create the plinth on either side of the *mihrab*. These surfaces are completely covered with luxuriant monochrome ornamentation which betrays a "dread of emptiness" (*horror vacui*) common in Islamic art. Such ornamentation reveals both prodigious virtuosity and great restraint, for the overall effect is of an almost abstemious unified surface.

Also around the remarkably rich *mihrab* and above the *alfiz* is an ornamental panel of seven small trefoil arches, supported by small columns. These arches frame beautiful floral motifs with a gold background, where vines and foliage bloom.

The Cupola

The roof which rises above the *maqsura* is undoubtedly the mosque's most interesting architectural and decorative element. Eight arches with slender, protruding interlocking ribs, inscribed in an octagonal plan 6 meters in diameter, support a ribbed cupola. These arches form a pattern which follows the principle of two interlocked squares, set at a 45 degree angle to each other – the same plan as in the Dome of the Rock in Jerusalem. This system of vaulting is the forerunner of the ribbed arches which were to revolutionize European architecture in the Gothic period.

This complex ceiling is completely covered with magnificent mosaics on a gold background – the work of Byzantine artists, as is the decoration of tesserae surrounding the *mihrab*. As in the Dome of the Rock and the Great Mosque of Damascus, artisans came from Constantinople to carry out the decoration at Cordoba. Caliph al-Hakam II received from the Byzantine emperor, *basileus* Nicephorus II Phocas (963–969), crews of mosaicists whose task was to create the gold decoration surrounding the mosque's "holy of holies".

These Christian artisans produced more abstract work than the depictions of landscapes which adorned the court of the Great Mosque of Damascus, because Constantinople had, since then, undergone two iconoclastic crises (730–787 and 815– 843). It seems that, having been criticized by the Muslims for disobeying the Biblical commandment forbidding the use of images, some Byzantine theologians had promoted the spread of iconoclastic principles.

Be that as it may, in Cordoba, no less than in the Near East, political situations and military events did not mar a fruitful artistic cooperation between the Umayyad caliphs and the Byzantine emperors. This point is important, for it

reveals a particular state of mind in the two religious communities – and one which was far from the fanaticism that later characterized relations between Muslims and Christians, both during the period of the Crusades and at the end of the *Reconquista* in Spain.

The Palace of Madinat al-Zahra

The emirs, and later the caliphs, of Cordoba had a "castle" which served as a palace: it was the Alcazaba, a fortress in which the sovereign lived with his personal guard. It seems that Cordoba's importance by the time of the accession of Abd al-Rahman III led the caliph to move outside the city for reasons of security, as several Roman emperors (such as Tiberius and Hadrian) had done.

We owe the construction of the palace complex of Madinat al-Zahra to the Caliph Abd al-Rahman III. It was built five kilometers from Cordoba over a period of five years, beginning in 936, and was not completed until the reign of al-Hakam II. This vast complex occupies a south-facing slope at the foot of "Bride's Mountain", within a rectangle surrounded by a wall measuring 1,500 by 750 meters. The regularity of this plan was not affected by the irregularity of the terrain, except to the north where there was a 70-meter drop towards the Guadalquivir River; here, the palace buildings were located, on terraces.

All the buildings of the palace at Madinat al-Zahra faced south, except for the mosque – which, along with its courtyard (completed in 940), faced south-west, and contained a hypostyle hall with seven naves delimited by porticoes perpendicular to the *qibla*. There was a series of courtyards or patios, usually square, surrounded by arcades and embellished by ornamental ponds. In the northern part, not far from the entrance, the main building used for the caliph's official receptions can be distinguished (though it is now in ruins). This quadrilateral of over 80 meters a side, with a central courtyard bordered by a portico, provided a sort of "Hall of Ambassadors." The building had five naves, each 40 meters wide, with a hypostyle hall for state occasions which was open to the south, and had a series of porticoes whose beautiful horseshoe arches had alternate red and white arch stones. This was probably the *Diwan i-Am*, or Public Palace, in contrast to the *Diwan i-Khas*, or Private Palace, described below.

The best restored part, thanks to the patient excavations of archeologists, is the private audience chamber, known as the "Abd al-Rahman III Room". This sumptuous reception room, whose appearance is closely related to the hypostyle space of the Great Mosque of Cordoba, had two arcades which divided the hall into three naves. Polychrome marble columns support large, alternating red and white arch stones, decorated with finely worked stucco. The flat ceiling was wooden, with raised beams in colors and gold. Marble decoration, identical to that of the *maqsura* of the Cordoba mosque, completely covered the walls.

In front of this throne room, which was 20 meters wide and entered through a transverse vestibule, was a spacious square pool of the same width. This entire complex lay in front of a royal pavilion placed in the middle of four pools, in a square garden supported by a terrace of 150 meters square. This green space, surrounding a pavilion and its pools, and built in the center of a plan with two axes, is related to the tradition of Abbasid palaces with their cruciform plans, called *chahr bagh* (four gardens). It was a true *paradeisos* or "paradise", having an aviary, a menagerie and arbors scattered throughout the greenery of the garden, with pools and fountains fed by an aqueduct supplied by mountain springs. These amenities created a sumptuous Garden of Eden around the all-powerful sovereign, whose glory was thereby exalted.

The scallop-shell motif
Inside the *mihrab* of the Great Mosque of Cordoba, the tiny space is topped with a scallop-shell motif – a decorative element dating from the late Roman Empire where it was often used above symbolic baldaquins.

Pages 100/101
Variations on the octagon
The two cupolas which flank the main dome of the Great Mosque of Cordoba have interlocking ribs dating from 961. A comparison with the illustration on page 103 below shows the similarities and differences between structures using this play of intersecting ribs. This cupola, to the right of the principal *mihrab,* is represented in the cross-section drawn by Girault de Prangey, reproduced on page 99.

Mosaic decoration
The entire "holy of holies" of the Great Mosque of Cordoba is covered with sumptuous Byzantine mosaics, from the arch of the *mihrab* (left), with its arch stones decorated with foliage on a red and gold background, to the area beneath the dome (right), with its inscriptions in large Kufic script between ribs, and the ribbed cupola.

Virtuosity of interlaced arches
The main cupola in front of the *mihrab* of the Great Mosque of Cordoba plays with Arabic geometrical structures and shimmering gold decoration made for al-Hakam II by mosaicists from Constantinople. The system of intersecting arches is based on the plan of two squares set at 45° angles to each other.

A transparent effect
The intersecting multifoil arches of the Great Mosque's *maqsura* create an effective boundary, while accentuating the richness of the place reserved for the caliph in front of the *mihrab*. The decoration has a symbolic role related to the power of the sovereign.

Decorative profusion

Finely carved marble decoration, with its motifs of symmetrical foliage, frames the *mihrab* of Cordoba, creating a vibrancy which expresses the *horror vacui* of Islamic art.

The *mihrab* of al-Hakam II

Surrounded by the *alfiz* which forms a projecting frame, a large horseshoe arch leads to the niche in the form of a blind room, in the *qibla* wall of the Great Mosque of Cordoba. This formula marks a specific stage of the *mihrab*'s development in Muslim architecture of the western empire. Above is a series of multifoil arches, with alternating light and dark arch stones, framed in mosaics depicting floral motifs on a gold background. Bands of inscriptions in Kufic script quote Koranic suras.

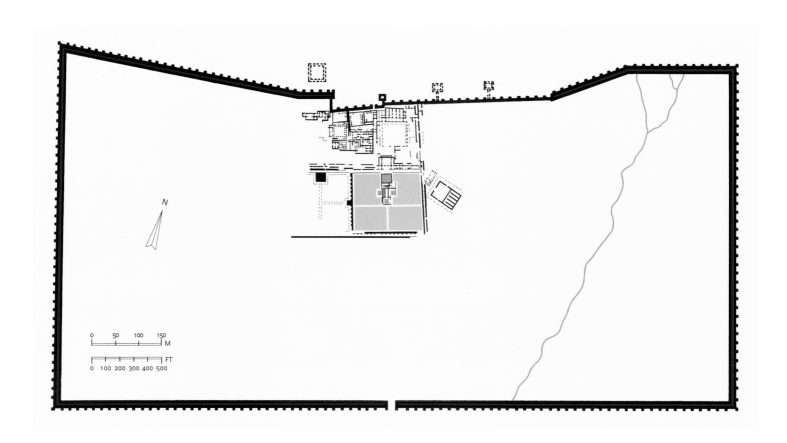

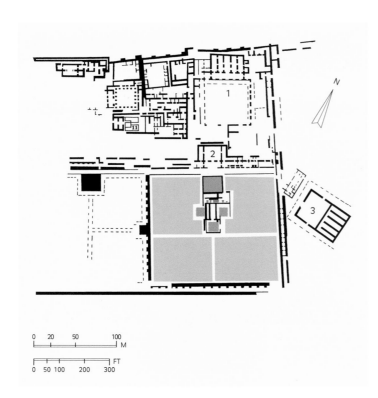

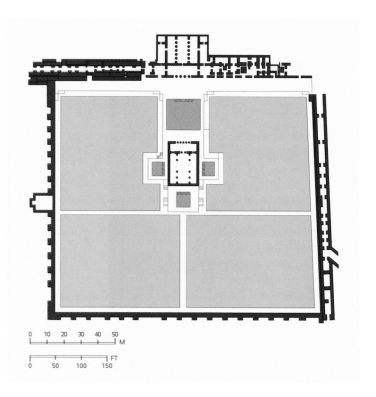

The palace-city of Madinat al-Zahra

Above: Plan of the caliph's stronghold, created by Abd al-Rahman III in 936, five kilometers from Cordoba. The walled city measures 1,500 meters long by 750 meters wide. The palace buildings occupy the upper area.

Below left: The palace quarter in the center of Madinat al-Zahra with, top, the *Diwan i-Am*, or public palace (1) and, below, the *Diwan i-Khas*, or private palace (2); to the right is the mosque, at an angle, thus oriented towards the Kaaba (3).

Below right: Detail of the private palace, with the "Abd al-Rahman III Room" in front of an ornamental pond leading to a *chahr bagh* garden, divided into four quadrants, in the Persian style, with a central pavilion and pools on each side.

Courtly grandeur
Crosswise view of the antechamber leading to the reception
hall of Abd al-Rahman III (on the
left). Palace architecture used
many of the same structural and
ornamental forms as the contemporary mosques.

Buildings to Enhance Prestige

Some idea of the extent of this palace-city, covering an area of 277 acres (112 hectares) can be gleaned by reading the works of Arab chroniclers. Al-Maqqari (died 1632), a later author who was a native of Tlemcen in Algeria and active in Cairo and Damascus, gathered together many medieval historical writings. He reported that the site at Madinat al-Zahra had required 6,000 ashlar blocks daily; these were transported by 800 camels and 1,000 mules. The columns used there (he claims) amounted to 4,315 marble shafts, some of which were imported from North Africa and even from Constantinople. He states that the caliphs appropri-ated annually the sum of 300,000 dinars for the construction of the palace (or the equivalent today of $ 500,000,000 in gold).

Some of the amenities of the palace are described by al-Maqqari, who refers to Ibn Hayyan of Cordoba, author of a chronicle of Abd al-Rahman III, between 912 and 942: "Among the marvels of Al-Zahra, there were two fountains with extra-ordinary basins. The larger of the two was from Constantinople, in gilded bronze, beautifully sculpted in bas-reliefs depicting people. The smaller one was of green marble (cipolin), from Syria. The caliph placed it in the exedra of his sitting room and surrounded it with golden statues of different animals."

Ibn Bashkuwal also describes the palace: "Among the marvels of Madinat al-Zahra [was] the Sitting Room of the Caliphs, the roof of which was in gold tile and translucent blocks of alabaster. On every side there were eight doors of ebony with gold highlights. Whenever the sun entered this room and al-Nasir [Abd al-Rahman III] wished to astonish his courtiers, he had only to make a sign to one of his slaves and the basin filled with mercury in the center of the room would move. The room itself seemed to turn, while the rays of light pierced the room frightening the assembly. It was the abundance of mercury in Spain which gave al-Nasir the idea for this mechanism which made the room seem to spin on itself, as on an axis. It seemed to follow the movement of the sun. The caliph was so concerned with the proper functioning of this mechanism, that he would allow only his son, al-Hakam, to oversee its maintenance."

The gardens, with their aviary and animals, and this room seeming to spin on its own axis, in harmony with the movement of the sun, is reminiscent of the cosmological palace of Nero, the *Domus Aurea* (Golden House) in Rome, containing a rotunda which, according to Suetonius, "continually revolved on its own axis, like the world". In the case of Madinat al-Zahra, we undoubtedly have a description from hearsay by an author who never saw the mechanism, and only half-understood its operation and function. It seems, indeed, that Ibn Hayyan's descriptions of the animal forms of the golden statues – lion, antelope, crocodile, eagle and dragon on one side, and dove, falcon, duck, kite and vulture on the other, "decorated with precious stones and spouting water" – derive from an imaginary jotted list of the "animals" of the zodiac and the constellations.

The device was surely a cosmological mechanism, able to turn because of the properties of the mercury contained in the basin. In this case, the "circle of animals" (a zodiac expression – from *zoon*, animal, living being – from ancient times) represented the celestial sphere, that is, the stars and planets. The caliph studied the stars to determine his horoscope, following a tradition formally recognized since Hellenistic times. The fact that only the crown prince could use this planetarium is reminiscent of the Roman prohibition, under pain of death, banning authors of horoscopes from serving anyone other than the prince, whose exclusive prerogative it was to resort to such an instrument.

Given these facts, it seems advisable to relegate this curious construction to the annals of cosmological thrones (in particular that of Khosrau II, studied by Herzfeld), of which Persian authors such as Thaalibi an-Naishaburi (961–1038) and Firdausi (932–1020), who were contemporary with the building of the palace of Madinat al-Zahra, gave extensive descriptions.

Thus the architectural remains of Madinat al-Zahra, seen in the light of these Persian-Arabic texts, take on a meaning that seemed to have been lost. Such reinterpretation helps us to focus on the extent of the astronomical and astrological machinery, and the advanced state of cosmological sciences, with their techniques of astral observation, which the Arabs of the early era inherited from the Greeks and Romans, and continued to develop. The treatises of al-Jazari (active around 1185) provide irrefutable testimony that this technology did actually exist.

The caliph's palace, with its courtyards created for public and private courtly rituals, represented a means of glorifying the sovereign. For their symbolic ceremonies, the caliphs of Andalusia consulted the stars, which contributed to the divinatory nature of the liturgies connected with power. All important decisions were taken with the assistance of astrologers, and no new city was founded without an astral consultation to determine its destiny. Caliph Abd al-Rahman III, who reigned between 912 and 961, was the exact contemporary of the Byzantine *basileus* (emperor) Constantine VII Porphyrogenitus (913–959), author of the well-known treatise entitled *The Book of Ceremonies,* a principal source of descriptions of the court rituals at Constantinople – a text with considerable influence in the Islamic world. The relations between the caliph and the *basileus* were such that the latter sent a delegation to Cordoba to offer the Arab a manuscript of Paulus

Imperial magnificence

The Caliph's Hall where, with great pomp and ceremony, the official guests of the powerful sovereign of Cordoba were received. The same architectural and ornamental principles are also used at Madinat al-Zahra, which characterized the sacred art of Cordoba: the same columns support horseshoe arches with large, alternating red and white voussoirs, the same flat ceilings and decorations chiseled in marble or stucco.

An oratory in Toledo
Built in 999, the small Umayyad
Mosque of Bib Mardun, known as
Cristo de la Luz (Christ of Light),
is like a cube with a frieze of interlaced arches on the façade. Its
rectangular plan is divided into
nine small squares.
Above right: Cross-section showing a tall building of small, juxta-
posed ribbed cupolas, each with a
different pattern of ribbing. From
an 1841 engraving by Girault de
Prangey.

Architectural dexterity

Above: The small dimensions of the Mosque of Bib Mardun in Toledo did not prevent the use of many types of vaulting, one for each of the nine divisions of the plan.

Below: Though the building is less than 8 meters a side, it has a large number of horseshoe arches linked together with reused columns from the prayer hall, whose complex spatial system recalls the Mosque of Cordoba.

The Origin of the Horseshoe Arch

A pre-Islamic formula
The horseshoe arch of the Visigoth church of San Juan de Baños (Palencia), dating from 661, shows that this form had existed in the Iberian peninsula at least fifty years before the arrival of the Arabs.

Power of a Moorish fortress
Page 112: The formidable citadel of Gormaz, with its high wall punctuated by twenty-four towers, dominates the course of the River Duero. It is one of the principal Arab strongholds of tenth-century Spain.
Below: Detail of the door opening into the outer bastion.

Arab builders are frequently credited with the invention of the horseshoe arch, for the simple reason that numerous Muslim buildings use this type of arch. However, the Visigoth monuments of Spain, dating from the seventh century A.D. (and thus predating Tariq's landing on the peninsula), use this form of construction between the Ebro and the Douro – for example, in the church of San Juan de Baños (661); while, in the Near East, a church such as that of Alahan, in Cilicia, has a few modest examples dating from A.D 560. Thus the horseshoe arch already existed in the imperial Roman era, and examples can also be found in Spanish funerary steles from the second and third centuries A.D. Thus the Arabs did not introduce the horseshoe arch to the West – but they did make extensive use of it, so that, from the eighth century, it became one of the distinctive features of their buildings.

Orosius, a Latin historian of Spanish origin, who had written a *History of the World*.

In the manner of the Constantinople ceremonies exalting the person of the emperor in the *sanctum palatium*, the Umayyad palace of Andalusia emphasized the sacred character of the person of the caliph. Hence it was important to use architectural surroundings and forms which symbolized the veneration felt towards the ruler, who was also Commander of the Faithful.

The Grandeur of the Abbasid Caliphate

Mesopotamia – Center of the Islamic World

Page 115
The wealth of the Abbasid caliphate
Brocades and samites, manufactured to an exceptionally high standard under Abbasid prerogative in Mesopotamia, Syria and Egypt, often copied Sassanid and Byzantine motifs. The weavers' workshops (or *tiraz*) were run according to strict rules. (Abegg Foundation, Riggisberg)

Stucco decoration in Samarra
Abbasid architecture in Mesopotamia used stucco for ornamental elements. These chiseled motifs, once polychrome, are from a ninth-century palace in Samarra; the hexagons are adorned with themes inspired by the vine, including grapes and foliage. (Baghdad Museum)

In 750, after the assassination of the entire Umayyad family of Damascus, one member escaped to Spain where he founded the Andalusian branch of the dynasty, which lasted with great distinction until 1031. The second dynasty of the Islamic empire was founded by Abu al-Abbas al-Saffah, a descendant of an uncle of the Prophet Muhammad, called Abbas, who lent his name to the dynasty. It lasted nominally for five centuries. In the beginning, between the eighth and the tenth centuries, the rulers were known as the Great Abbasids, for they reigned mightily, exercising their powers to the full. Later Abbasids ruled with merely symbolic authority, based on the religious prestige of the title of caliph.

As a result of the progressive fragmentation of the territories under his authority, the Abbasid caliph soon reigned over no more than Mesopotamia, Syria and a part of Persia. After the Muslim emancipation of Spain, there was a series of secessions. These included Ifriqiya under the Aghlabids in 800, Khurasan under the Tahirids in 830, Egypt under the Tulunids in 868, and finally western Persia under the Buyid emirs. The Buyids were sufficiently powerful to place Abbasid caliphs in effective tutelage, which marked the end of the sumptuous period of the rule of the Great Abbasids.

But the two centuries during which this highly developed culture blossomed – progressing architecturally from the Round City of Baghdad to the new city of Samarra – unquestionably marked the apogee of Islamic power and influence. The caliph was an absolute monarch commanding both army and government. He introduced policies and was the guardian of the faith. He was a sacred sovereign, surrounded by a court made up of a multitude of Arab princes and aristocrats, courtiers, ministers, counselors and artists. He was the center of a complex and sumptuous courtly ritual, which was the admiration of foreign visitors and ambassadors. At his side, the vizier, or mayor of the palace, acted as "prime minister".

One profound influence on the fortunes of the Abbasid dynasty was the presence of a powerful garrison of Turks, who replaced the forces from Khurasan, to form the caliph's "Praetorian guard". Recently converted to Islam, these soldiers were a turbulent element, always ready to rebel or provoke incidents with the Arab-Persian population. But the caliph needed such a strike force to quell the attempted "coups d'état" threatening his authority. The presence of this formidable corps of mercenaries affected town planning and the design of the palace: if they were too near the palace, the Turks posed a danger for the caliph, should he be unable to confine them to their barracks; yet if they were too far away, the ruler was at the mercy of a "putsch". This dilemma posed a particular problem as a result of the configuration of the city of Baghdad, and a satisfactory solution was never found.

In Khurasan – where the partisans of Ali (the Alids or Shiites) were numerous – there were uprisings which led to the accession of the Abbasids. Abu Muslim also established himself there, later identified by the Shiites as the *mahdi*, the hidden *imam*, who was supposed to return to earth at the end of time, according to an eschatological Persian concept. But after the victory won by the insurgents, members of the Prophet Muhammad's family proclaimed Abu al-Abbas caliph; he reigned in Kufa under the name of al-Saffah, meaning "The Bloodthirsty". The Shiites, who had contributed significantly to the establishment of the new dynasty, were frustrated in their hopes of coming to power.

The impetus for the change came from the east, and from this time onwards, the eastern part of the Islamic empire was to be at the forefront of its development. With the Abbasids, the Muslim world turned away somewhat from the Byzantine influences which had predominated under the Umayyads. Now, it was the heritage of the Sassanid empire that fuelled the caliph's culture, government and court life. This Persian influence contributed to an acceptance of the divine nature of the royal power incarnate in the Abbasid caliphs, following the example of the Sassanid King of Kings. It led to the exaltation of courtly ritual, whose liturgy blossomed throughout the palace. More than ever, the purpose of art was to glorify the sovereign.

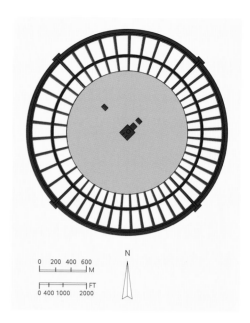

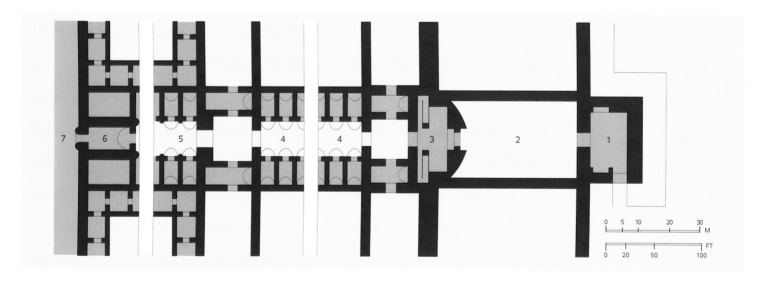

Al-Mansur's Baghdad

From 754 to 775, al-Mansur, "the Victorious", was caliph. In 762 he founded a new capital called Baghdad, the "City of Salvation", on the banks of the Tigris. Built on a fertile alluvial plain where there was no stone for construction, the city of the caliphs was constructed completely of sun-dried bricks, each measuring 50 by 50 centimeters, and baked-brick structures. Because of this, and also because the site has been continually occupied since then, there is no trace of the caliph's city. This is characteristic of Mesopotamia where huge conurbations have completely disappeared. However, we know about Baghdad's appearance from the admiring accounts and descriptions by Arab authors, in particular al-Khatib.

Its plan was that of a "Round City", a name by which it was often called. Both the site, near the ancient Sassanid capital of Ctesiphon, and the date for starting the building work, were determined by astrologers and geomancers. In following cosmological considerations that dated back to the Assyrians, they drew a circular plan whose origins lay in the cities of Nineveh, Hatra, Haran and Firuzabad. Baghdad's outermost diameter was 2.6 kilometers. Three concentric walls protected the city: between the first, which had 112 towers, and the second was a glacis or incline, while between the second and the third walls stood different districts of the city. In this ring-shaped area, radial streets divided the residential area into 45 sections.

The Baghdad of al-Mansur
Known for its opulence, the Round City of Baghdad, founded on a circular plan in 762 by Caliph al-Mansur, had avenues bordered with bazaars radiating from the center, in which stood the caliph's palace and the principal mosque surrounded by gardens.
Above: Overall plan.
Below: Detail of the concentric walls surrounding the city districts along a radial avenue leading to the center:
1. Outer bastion
2. Guard house
3. Fortified gate
4. Rows of shops
5. Second row of shops
6. Gateway to the gardens
7. Gardens surrounding the palace and the Great Mosque

Two concentric enclosures

Plan of the Ukhaidir Palace, whose outer enclosure has a double symmetry with two axes. A second wall surrounds the palace itself, which has a rectangular plan, offset to the north. For security reasons, Isa ibn Musa, who lived under the terrible Harun al-Rashid, overlooked no defensive element:

1. Main gate
2. Secondary gates
3. Vaulted vestibule
4. Mosque
5. Courtyard for state occasions
6. Reception hall, or *aula palatina* (palace hall)
7. Apartments with courtyards
8. Outbuilding

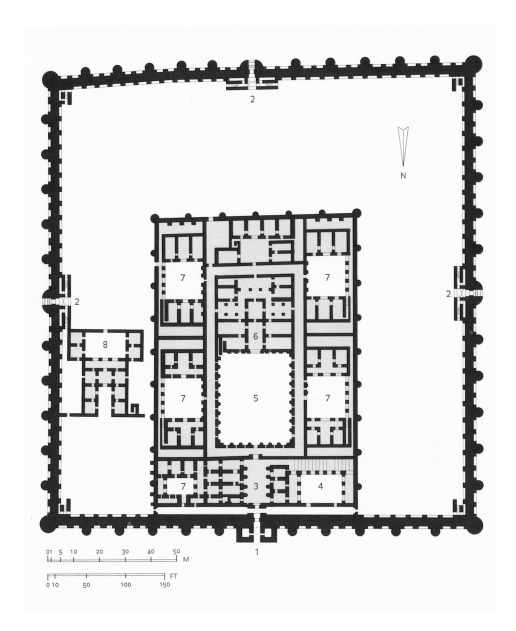

The princely palace of Ukhaidir

In the Mesopotamian desert stands the fortified enclosure of Ukhaidir. Constructed in 778, its mass is punctuated by round towers and arches concealing machicolations; the fortifications enclose a palace complex built in stone masonry.

Strong fortifications
Behind the outermost walls, arcades support the parapet walk giving access to loopholes and machicolations.

A series of courtyards
Inside the inner wall, the Ukhaidir Palace has a series of apartments opening on to courtyards and luxurious open spaces separating the state rooms.

Page 121
The mighty gateways
This gate to the Ukhaidir Palace, in the form of a projecting tower, uses state-of-the-art siege defenses: portcullis, machicolations, guardhouses above the entrance, etc.

Four gates gave access to the city. These were located on the bisectors of the four cardinal points – to the south-west, the south-east, the north-west and the north-east – corresponding to the great regions of the empire: Arabia, Syria, Kirman and Khurasan. Long, vaulted, covered bazaars were erected along these four entrance axes, starting from the fortified gates.

The central area was occupied by an immense circular park measuring 1,500 meters in diameter. In the middle stood the palace and, beside it, the Great Mosque. This palace, called Dar al-Khilafa, formed a square 200 x 200 meters in size. A green cupola, called Qubba al-Khadra, 40 meters high and covered with enameled bricks, dominated the whole. It was flanked by four large *iwans*. The *iwan*, a creation of Parthian Sassanid Persia, was a kind of throne room – a huge vaulted hall with an open façade which lent itself to the sovereign's ritual appearances. Later it was adopted in mosques as a vestibule to the prayer hall. The cruciform plan of the palace in the heart of Baghdad was inherited from the palace of Abu Muslim in Merv, which in turn was derived from the large Sassanid palaces, in particular from the palace in Ctesiphon.

The Great Mosque of Baghdad, which adjoined the palace, measured 100 meters on each side and had a square courtyard. It was enlarged in the reign of Harun al-Rashid (786–809). Nothing remains of this immense Abbasid creation, just as nothing remains of the Babylonian and Assyrian cities, which, after the ravages of war, literally crumbled to dust, especially when the site was abandoned or when the capital was moved. This process can be seen in the successive foundations of Rusafa, by al-Mahdi (775–786), and later in the walls by al-Musta'in (862–866) and by al-Mustazhir (1092–1118).

A Persian-style door-frame
The vaulted entrance (or *pishtaq*), an important element in Persian architecture, is used at Ukhaidir. This high, flat door-frame was used in Near Eastern architecture, and later in all Islamic buildings, whether religious or secular.

The Fortified Palace of Ukhaidir

About 120 kilometers south of the Round City, outside the Mesopotamian basin, are the ruins of a vast fortified palace complex called Ukhaidir, or the "Green". This complex, the only desert palace known from the Abbasid period, was located inside a line of defense measuring 635 by 531 meters. It consisted of an inner enclosure, 175 x 169 meters, within which was a second wall, 112 x 82 meters, enclosing the palace itself. This construction, dating from 778, which can be seen in its arid surroundings today, was originally at the heart of a vast agricultural estate, amply irrigated by a diversion of the Tigris. It is thought to have been the work of Isa ibn Musa, nephew of al-Mansur, who was ousted by Harun al-Rashid.

This monumental palace was constructed, not in brick, but with rough quarry-stones held together by mortar – doubtless because of the abundance of available stone on the site of Ukhaidir, at the southern edge of the Mesopotamian plain. Stone may also have been chosen due to its greater strength – desirable for a fortified enclosure. Indeed, security seems to have been of primary importance for Isa ibn Musa, who feared an attempt on his life by the caliph. Thus there were forty-four semicircular towers around the walls, which contained four fortified gates, and a parapet walk with machicolations – a technical innovation already used on a smaller scale in the Umayyad palace of Kasr al-Hayr. Inside this inner enclosure, the palace itself was defended by twenty towers abutting its walls.

A soaring vault
The large entrance hall of the Ukhaidir Palace has a powerful ogival arched vault, supported on stronge embedded cylindrical columns. This system anticipates early western Romanesque art by more than 200 years.

This strictly rectangular, symmetrical organization was related to the Umayyad palaces of Syria and Palestine – although the plan of Ukhaidir was not ruled by the cardinal points, nor by a *decumanus*, as was the city of Anjar, for example. The palace was offset toward the north and literally abutted the northern enclosing wall. The projecting postern gate on the nothern wall opened on to a transversal vaulted corridor used by the guards; behind this was a monumental anteroom, known as the Great Hall. This hall was covered with a centrally ribbed, slightly pointed vault in brick, on stone-work arcades, supported by large cylindrical columns. The arches perpendicular to the nave formed a buttress to the vault. The overall heavy and powerful appearance is reminiscent of buildings of the early Romanesque period, which were to appear in the West two centuries later.

The Great Hall opened axially on to the main courtyard, 35 meters long by 28 meters wide, which in turn led to a large *iwan* where a palace ritual must have taken place, which, if not matching the pomp of the caliphs, must nevertheless have been inspired by it. To the right, before the entrance to the courtyard, there was a mosque (compare the palace of Mshatta); this consisted of an oblong hall with a single bay, preceded by a courtyard with, on three sides, a portico of round columns in stuccoed masonry. Surrounding the official palace (the courtyard, the *iwan* and reception halls) were five dwellings with small courtyards, creating apartments with six rooms. Between the palace and the wall, a single building broke the symmetry of the whole: this was an annex whose plan echoed that of the official central part, but which was situated on the eastern side. It may have been an addition for one of Isa ibn Musa's children.

The princely mosque
To the right of the entrance to the Ukhaidir Palace is a small mosque, its courtyard surrounded by thick, cylindrical columns supporting vaulted arcades which form the prayer hall (above). Its oblong space is covered with a barrel vault decorated with abstract motifs in stucco work (opposite).

The last vestiges of a great metropolis
The Abbassid capital, founded on the Tigris in 836 by Caliph al-Mutasim and abandoned in 892, was built entirely of brick, mostly sun-baked. The gigantic conurbation, 25 kilometers long, literally melted away, leaving only ghostly traces of vanished streets and buildings, which can be seen in this aerial view.

The New Capital in Samarra

The plan of the Round City of Baghdad had great disadvantages: it could not grow in response to need; and there was no practical site for the barracks of the Turkish troops who formed the caliph's personal guard and who, since the time of al-Mutasim (833–842), had completely replaced the troops from Khurasan. These difficulties prompted al-Mansur's successors to construct a new capital 100 kilometers to the north-west, also on the river Tigris. It was al-Mutasim who decided,

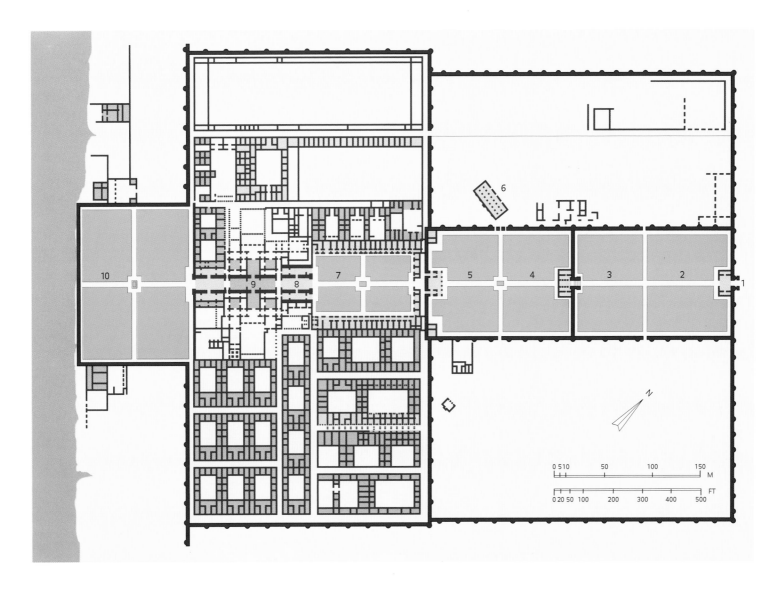

The caliph's magnificent palace
Plan of the Bulkawara Palace in Samarra, built between 850 and 860 on the south bank of the Tigris by the Abbasid ruler, al-Mutawakkil. The city with walls 2.4 kilometers in circumference, is entered along the main symmetrical axis (from right to left) through two rectangular gardens arranged in *chahr bagh* style, and a large courtyard. This leads to a cruciform, central audience chamber beyond which there is another garden overlooking the Tigris:

1. Main gate
2. First garden
3. Second gate
4. Second garden
5. Third gate
6. Palace mosque
7. Main courtyard
8. Vestibule
9. Cruciform *aula regia*
10. Garden overlooking the Tigris

in 836, to settle in Samarra with his court and government. Rejecting the formula of an enclosed city, he chose to construct a series of walled districts along the river. These varied constructions ended up forming a conurbation almost thirty-five kilometers long and between two and five kilometers wide which, during its fifty or so years of active use (836–883), probably had more than 500,000 inhabitants (at a time when Paris, for example, contained barely 30,000).

Like Baghdad, little remains of this city, even though the site of Samarra was not reoccupied after its abandonment by the Caliph al-Mutamid. It contained the two largest mosques in the Islamic world, and its palaces were vast: the Palace of Bulkawara, built by Mutawakkil, covered 89 acres (36 hectares), while the earlier Jausaq al-Kharqani, built by al-Mutasim, covered about 370 acres (150 hectares). Here again, the building material was sun-dried brick, with ornamentation and vaults of baked brick and highlights of carved and painted stucco.

The scale of these buildings was enormous. The more recent and smaller of these two Samarran palaces, that of Bulkawara, had a central axis 800 meters long, commanding symmetrical structures enclosed with walls and punctuated by 160 semicircular towers. The plan included advancing 300 meters towards the Tigris. The axis first crossed two four-part gardens in the form of Persian *chahr baghs*, preceded by monumental gates with *iwans*. It then led to the main body of the building, surrounded by a wall 460 meters wide and 100 meters long. This contained the residential area, with dwellings with small courtyards, following the traditional local custom, a recurrent formula governing the dwellings of the different members of the caliph's retinue.

The vaulting system
The barrel vaults of the gateway of the Jausaq al-Kharqani Palace in Samarra, in the form of an *iwan*, end in pendentives.

In the center rose the official palace, its ceremonial halls preceded by a large courtyard bordered with porticoes, which led to a cruciform structure. In its center was a cupola buttressed by four *iwans*, in the Sassanid manner. Beyond this *aula regia*, was another four-part garden in the form of the *chahr bagh*, whose terrace overlooked the river.

In this magnificent complex, there were halls lined with paneling in precious woods, walls covered with carved stucco, and polychrome paintings decorating the halls of the harem, depicting hunting scenes and young, semi-nude women bathing (for although the ban on representational images was respected in places of prayer, such was not the case in the palace). In the halls and in the park, an irrigation system circulated water, giving a feeling of freshness. Waterspouts and bubbling fountains, aquatic mirrors reflecting the façades covered with mirrors of mother-of-pearl or white marble – all created a feeling of ethereal delicacy in this palace of a "thousand and one nights".

This beguiling quality is emphasized by chroniclers, who mentioned a series of remarkable mechanical devices which were displayed on the occasion of the

Gateway on the river
Of the enormous Jausaq al-Kharqani Palace, constructed in 836 by al-Mutasim in Samarra and measuring 1.5 kilometers in length, all that remains is this monumental triple arcade of pointed brick arches, which opens on to the Tigris.

Carved decorations
The scarcity of stone in the alluvial plain of Mesopotamia means that the decoration of the Samarra palaces is mostly in stucco with recurrent motifs which cover the plinths of the brick walls. (Baghdad Museum)

A Sassanid palace
The palace of Ctesiphon near Baghdad is a monument to the magnificence of the Sassanids, whom the Islamic forces conquered. This building has an immense arch, 36 meters high, made entirely of brick. It marks the apogee of a sixth-century technique of elliptical roofing, which was a source of inspiration to Muslim architects.

Byzantine ambassadors' visit to Baghdad in 917, when they presented their respects to al-Muktadir (908–932). Dominique Sourdel quotes the following description: "[On the caliph's orders] a tree rose out of the earth with different movements, filling the cupola and spouting streams of rosewater and musk water, while figures of birds sang in its branches."

In order to understand these Islamic palaces, built in the form of walled cities, we must recognize the role of gardens in this architecture, which is also a form of town planning. In this country of deserts (Mesopotamia was permanently arid unless it was artificially irrigated), all gardens were walled to protect the plants from hot, sandy winds. The formula of a man-made park, divided into four parts by water channels, corresponds, as we have mentioned, to the *chahr bagh* of the Persians. This enclosed garden is called "paradise" in Persian, and is based on the millennial, cosmological belief which identified paradise with the Garden of Eden and its four rivers. In their palace gardens, sovereigns attempted to reproduce this image, also depicting the different kingdoms of living things: the plant world, with flowers and trees producing exotic oils; the animal world, with birds in

aviaries next to fish in ponds and wild or domesticated animals raised in vast "reserves". The overall design followed an Achaemenid and Hellenistic tradition, and was the ancestor of our botanical and zoological gardens.

Furthermore, the quadripartite system extended to all architecture. That is why the palace plan followed this rectangular pattern, which also ruled all urban planning. The only element that did not obey this imperative was the palace mosque, which was off-center in relation to the other buildings, in order to obey religious imperatives that imposed an orientation towards the Kaaba.

The Two Great Mosques of Samarra

It was in their mosques that the Abbasid taste for the large-scale reached its culmination in Samarra. The Great Mosque, built by Caliph al-Mutawakkil between 848 and 852, looked from the outside like a fortified enclosure punctuated by forty-four semicircular towers. This high wall, measuring 240 by 156 meters, enclosed an area of 10 acres (4 hectares). It was in turn surrounded by two enclosures – the exterior one, measuring 440 by 376 meters, formed the *ziyada*, an area of quiet separating the place of prayer from the bustle of the surrounding city. Inside the wall, which contained fourteen gates, there was a courtyard of 160 by 110 meters, with porticoes on all four sides. There were three rows of supports on the north side, four to the east and west, and nine to the south, forming the *haram*. The prayer hall thus contained twenty-five naves of nine bays each, or 216 supports, providing an immense covered space of almost 10,000 square meters. The sides were made up of 168 columns and the portico to the north of 72, making a total of 456 rectangular columns separated by four small corner columns. A wooden roof of teak rested directly on top of these supports, without any arcades.

This was a relatively improvised architectural system, whose rough aspect was mitigated by its grandiose dimensions. It was made of baked brick – a luxury compared to the sun-dried brick used, for example, for the palaces. Furthermore, the pillar columns were stuccoed. The area of the *mihrab* must have had a sumptuous covering, using such precious materials as faïence tiles, and encrustations of mother-of-pearl and ivory, etc.

The minaret – called Malwiya, or "snail-shell" – was perhaps the most spectacular example of Abbasid architecture. Placed on the longitudinal axis, to the north of the enclosure, it rose opposite the wall of the *qibla*. This minaret, which stood 55 meters high, was in the form of a round step-like tower around which a spiral

A vast mosque
The Great Mosque of Samarra, built between 848 and 852 by al-Mutawakkil, looks like a fortress: its high wall, with forty-four semicircular towers, measures 160 by 110 meters, and encloses the largest prayer area of Islam. Built of brick, it has lost its hypostyle hall which had 216 octagonal supports and was covered with a flat, wood-framed roof.

Page 131
An Islamic "Ziggurat"
The immense brick minaret called the Malwiya (or "snail-shell"), whose spiral ramp rises above the Great Mosque of Samarra to a height of 55 meters. Its curious form derives from Babylonian ziggurats, whose techniques of construction it copied from thousands of years before.

Monumental severity
Elevation and plan of the Malwiya minaret of Samarra's Great Mosque, which combines a simplicity of principle with a perfection of technical realization in a humble material.

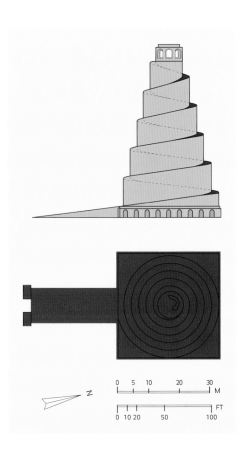

Like a scroll unwinding …
This aerial view shows Malwiya's curious form. To issue his call to prayer, five times a day the muezzin of Samarra had to climb the spiral ramp of this minaret, whose brick mass dominated the ninth-century Abbasid capital.

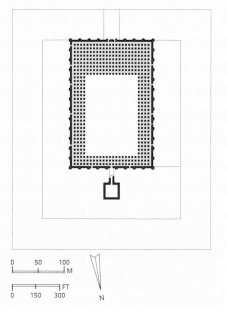

A grandiose plan
The Great Mosque of Samarra was surrounded by two walls forming the *ziyada*, or buffer zone protecting the prayer hall from the city's bustle. The outer wall covered an area of 470 by 400 meters, or almost 50 acres. The building had a hypostyle hall, with large porticoes around the courtyard; to the north was the spiral minaret.

**The spiral minaret
at Abu Dulaf**
The second large mosque in
Samarra, in the Abu Dulaf quarter,
had the same form as the Malwiya,
though its proportions were
smaller.

**The enclosure of the
Abu Dulaf Mosque**
In 859, Caliph al-Mutawakkil built
another huge mosque in Samarra,
in the Abu Dulaf district. This aerial view reveals considerable evid-
ence of the prayer hall and the
surrounding wall which measured
213 by 135 meters.

ramp led to the top. It evoked the image of the "Tower of Babel" and Babylonian ziggurats, with their access on inclined planes. This resemblance illustrates the continuity of solutions which the use of brick as a building material dictated in Mesopotamia.

In the north-western area of Samarra, al-Mutawakkil decided in 847 to build a new district called Abu Dulaf. There he built another gigantic mosque which also had a spiral minaret, though less colossal. Inaugurated in 861, this building had a prayer hall surrounded by a wall with towers at intervals along its length. Measuring 213 by 135 meters, it was almost as vast as that of the Great Mosque. But at Abu Dulaf, the *haram* had great brick arcades resting on rectangular pillars, which showed some progress from the architectural point of view. The prayer hall had seventeen naves and five bays; starting from the *mihrab*, two more bays were added, which were wider and supported by transverse pillars. This system made a T-formation, with the emphasis on the principal nave, characteristic of many hypostyle mosques in Egypt, Kairouan and the Maghreb.

The use of arcades
Unlike the Great Mosque of Samarra, which had octagonal pillars supporting a wooden roof, the Abu Dulaf Mosque had sixteen brick arcades forming naves perpendicular to the *qibla*. The building material created heavy structures, and square pillars support the arches, preventing an overall view of the spaces inside.

The Birth of Funerary Architecture

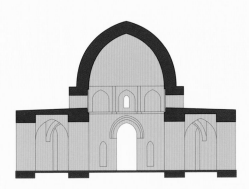

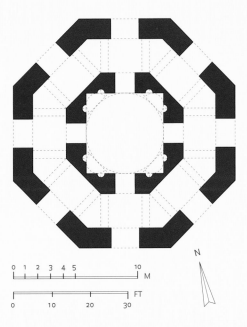

0 1 2 3 4 5   10   M

0   10   20   30   FT

The first Islamic mausoleum
Elevation and plan of the tomb of Caliph al-Muntasir in Samarra, called the Qubba al-Sulaybiya and dating from 862. This octagonal building was covered with a cupola, and had an ambulatory around the funerary hall for circumambulation.

The building of an elaborate funerary monument commemorating a deceased person violated the egalitarian principles of early Islam. The first known mausoleum in a Muslim country was built in Samarra, on the south bank of the Tigris, facing the Jausaq al-Kharqani palace. It was the Qubba al-Sulaybiya, an octagonal monument with an ambulatory surrounding a square funerary hall, and a cupola 6.3 meters in diameter. This was the tomb of Caliph al-Muntasir, who died in 862, and whose mother, a Greek Orthodox Christian, had obtained permission to have a tomb built for her son. Later the Caliphs al-Mutazz (died 869) and al-Muhtadi (died 870) were also entombed here.

From its plan, it seems that the Qubba al-Sulaybiya derived its inspiration from the Dome of the Rock (Qubba al-Sakhra) of Jerusalem, as well as from Byzantine shrines. The existence of a vaulted ambulatory shows that the rite of circumambulation was practiced, and its appropriation by the caliphs thus shows their desire to emphasize the sovereign's sacred nature. The building was constructed from artificial stone molded into a brick-like form, each piece being 33 centimeters square and 10 centimeters thick. It was probably covered with stucco and precious materials.

Thus at Samarra, for the first time, a tomb for Islamic princes was built, a formula which was to enjoy an extraordinary expansion and uncommon pomp. Masterpieces such as the Persian *gombads*, the Turkish *turbehs*, the tombs of the caliphs of Cairo and the mausoleums of Mogul India all followed in this tradition.

THE DIVERSITY OF MUSLIM EGYPT

From the Sunni Sultans to the Fatimid Caliphs

Page 137
Scientific advances
Classical Islam contributed greatly both to the preservation of the ancient scientific heritage and to the development of knowledge. The astrolabe is one of the instruments that Muslim scholars continued to improve, both for astronomical observations essential for navigation on the high seas, and for composing horoscopes, for astrology played an important part in the rule of Arab sovereigns.

Cairo's first mosque
The Amr Mosque, founded by general Amr ibn al-As in 642, in Fustat, the precursor of Cairo. Altered and enlarged several times, the Amr Mosque had a hypostyle hall which gave it its nickname, "the mosque with 400 columns". An engraving by Louis Mayer, dating from 1802, showing the building in a state of ruin.

Coptic and Monophysite Egypt, living under the oppression of the Orthodox Byzantines, greeted the Muslim conquerors as liberators. From the beginning of the Islamic era the country had been a splendid crossroads of spiritual influences and movements – a diversity manifested in its architectural masterpieces.

The first Egyptian mosque was built at Fustat, a city founded by the Arabs at the time of the conquest, in 641, on a site near Cairo (the new capital that the Fatimids were to build later). This mosque bears the name of Amr ibn al-As, a victorious general who, in 642, started work on the building, the appearance of which changed many times during its long history. It was demolished and rebuilt in 698, rebuilt again in 711, enlarged in 750, and again in 791.

The Amr Mosque finally attained its present dimensions in 827, when Abd Allah ibn Tahir gave it its final form. This checkered gestational period reveals not only the uncertainties of the architects attempting to establish the classic prototype of the mosque during the first two centuries of the Hegira, but also the rapid growth of the number of Muslims wishing to pray in a congregational hall large enough to house many worshippers.

A knowledge of the origins of this building's structure is essential to understanding why it underwent so many alterations. It was an architectural feat, with its construction of reused columns and capitals forming porticoes perpendicular to the *qibla*, with arches constructed out of light stonework. These elements were joined together, at the level of the imposts, by wooden tie rods which ran crosswise and lengthwise to form a lofty, rectangular structure. This system, which crisscrossed the space, provided effective braces and gave the whole structure a certain rigidity.

The Amr Mosque, which covered an area of about 120 by 110 meters and was related to the early versions of the mosques in Cordoba and Kairouan, was thus a typical example of the hypostyle house of prayer. It was composed of about twenty naves and had 150 columns. The oblong space of the *haram* was preceded by a courtyard, in the center of which was the fountain for ritual ablutions.

The Nilometer of Roda: A Municipal Building

The reigns of the Great Abbasids were marked by considerable technical progress. As long as the caliphs held sway in Egypt, they concerned themselves with agricultural yields. This desire to develop the necessary technology for exploiting irrigated land was characteristic of Mesopotamian sovereigns, whose wealth depended in large measure on the irrigation systems of the Mesopotamian plain.

In Egypt, where conditions were similar, al-Mutawakkil (847–861) built a Nilometer, conceived along the lines of the administrative buildings of the pharaohs. Built in 861, it occupied the southernmost point of the isle of Roda, facing Old Cairo. This subterranean building demonstrated an advanced level of scientific knowledge. It was in the form of a square well, in ashlar, using an elaborate system of stone cutting, and with remarkably elegant pointed arches. Vaulted

niches helped to strengthen the structure, withstanding the lateral thrust exerted on the walls – for this building went down about 12 meters into the ground. The building was in three sections, each one narrower than the one before, going down to the lowest level of the course of the Nile. A stairway descended to the base of the well, where two tunnels led to the water.

In the center of the building was a beautiful, graduated octagonal column, allowing a reading of the maximum level reached by the Nile spates. The number indicated on the shaft was used by the caliph to assess annual taxes on rural properties. According to Arab authors, the Nilometer of Roda, whose technique was based on the principle of communicating vessels, was the product of a collaboration between the architect Ahmad ibn Muhammad al-Hasib and the celebrated mathematician, al-Farghani. The work may have been completed by Sultan Ahmad ibn Tulun who seized power in Egypt in 868.

From the reign of Caliph al-Mutazz of Samarra (866–869), the Abbasid empire was increasingly jolted by revolutionary movements. These included the revolt of the Zanj, black slaves on the sugar plantations of south-western Mesopotamia, who were led by an Alid pretender; the uprising of the Carmathians of Syria and eastern Arabia, stirred up by Ismaili Shiites; and the rebellion of the Saffarids in Seistan and then Khurasan, whom the Samanids suppressed at the beginning of the tenth century. It was in the midst of these upheavals that general Ahmad ibn Tulun's succession took place. Of Turkish origin, born in Samarra and the son of a slave from Bukhara, ibn Tulun was made governor of Egypt and Syria in the name of Caliph al-Mutazz.

When he declared himself independent, no longer recognizing central Abbasid power, his revolt provoked no reaction; Baghdad merely noted the secession of one of its wealthiest provinces.

The courtyard façade
The Amr Mosque in Cairo underwent a series of alterations, attaining its largest dimensions in 827. Its hypostyle hall was bordered with light arcades facing the courtyard. Ancient reused columns supported the porticoes, which were perpendicular to the *qibla*.

The typical hypostyle hall
The Amr Mosque's light and lofty structure – with wooden tie rods linking the imposts – is typical of early Islamic prayer halls, with arcades supported by columns taken from Roman Byzantine monuments.

Ibn Tulun and Abbasid Techniques

From his palace of al-Qatai, ibn Tulun ruled his country with authority. The memory of vast mosques, constructed in brick in the Mesopotamian tradition, had remained with him from Samarra, where he grew up. Thus he decided to erect in Fustat (near the future site of Cairo) a similar house of prayer of monumental proportions. Since the time of the pharaohs, stone had typically been used for temples and tombs in the Nile valley; but ibn Tulun preferred the brick construction and stucco decoration used in Mesopotamia.

The Great Mosque of ibn Tulun was started in 876 and completed by 879. While not matching the dimensions of the Samarra mosque, it was nevertheless an innovation in Egypt because of its size. A square outer wall enclosed the *ziyada* (162 meters a side, covering an area of 6.4 acres or 2.6 hectares). The mosque itself measured 140 by 116 meters and included, in the center, a square courtyard measuring 90 x 90 meters, with arcaded porticoes along all four sides. The oblong prayer hall was about three times wider than it was deep. It was made up of five bays parallel to the *qibla* and totaled eighty transverse columns supporting identical pointed arches. These arcades were slightly horseshoe-shaped, meeting at a height of 8.1 meters. The rhythm of these regular porticoes continued without a break for the length of the double gallery encircling the three other sides of the courtyard, which was composed of eighty more pillars. These had embedded small columns at the corners, while the arcades and the intrados of the arches were covered with motifs in molded and carved stucco, as in the Samarran palaces. Between the arches, a bay was inserted into the spandrel; this lightened the portico visually, and also strengthened the structure. Ibn Tulun's mosque had a spiral minaret of brick, also in the Samarran tradition. This was later rebuilt in stone, probably at the time of the Mamluks, when the central fountain of the courtyard

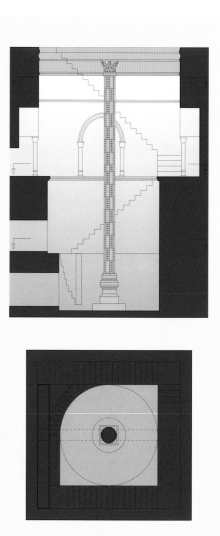

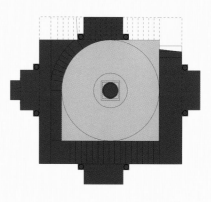

was also rebuilt during the restoration of the venerable building, which by then was 400 years old. In 1877, the collapse of a series of arcades in the prayer hall required further restoration, which was undertaken in 1929.

The Mosque of ibn Tulun was a masterpiece remarkable for its plan and unity of conception. Furthermore, it helps us to imagine the appearance of the great mosques of Samarra, which are now too ruined to offer an accurate picture of their roofed areas. Because of its considerable size, this building emphasized the horizontal nature of its proportions. Apart from the minaret, the only vertical feature of this quadrilateral was the brick cupola which rose above the *mihrab*. This was an innovation, and a departure from the style of the Great Mosque of Samarra. The formula of arcades parallel (rather than perpendicular) to the *qibla*, and the use of broad pillars, restricted lines of sight towards the *mihrab*, and produced a stark,

A building to measure water-levels
The Nilometer of Roda was constructed in ninth-century Cairo on an island in the Nile. This subterranean building was used to measure the river level in order to establish the tax rate. Built around a central, graduated column, the stone building formed a deep well linked to the Nile. *Above right:* Cross-section and plan of the Nilometer of Roda.

The Nilometer of Roda
A view of the Nilometer by Louis Mayer, dating from the early nineteenth century, when the instrument was still in use.

The continuity of science
The Nilometer was built of courses of large dressed stones, its interior appearance reflecting its technical requirements. The tall polygonal column is held in place by a beam covered with Kufic inscriptions. This work of the Abbasid period, probably completed by Ahmad ibn Tulun, illustrates the Muslim rulers' desire to continue the scientific traditions of ancient Egypt.

Ibn Tulun's masterpiece

General Ahmad ibn Tulun built a mosque in Fustat, between 876 and 879, after he had assumed the reins of power in Egypt. It was one of the largest Islamic buildings in the Nile valley, measuring 140 by 160 meters and including a *ziyada*, or exterior courtyard, which isolated the mosque from its busy surroundings, as seen in this aerial view.

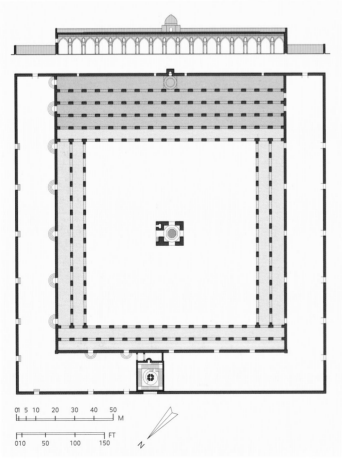

A disciplined structure

Elevation and plan of Ibn Tulun's mosque in Fustat, with its surrounding courtyard, or *ziyada*. The hypostyle has five bays whose arcades are parallel to the *qibla*. All the porticoes are built on the same model.

severe appearance. This was tempered by light stucco motifs adorning the capitals and the borders of the arches, as well as the geometrical tracery of the screens in front of the high windows. The motifs carved in the wooden doors and timberwork were probably the work of Coptic carpenters. In addition, at the edges of the terrace covering the prayer hall and the porticoes of the courtyard, was an elegant openwork balustrade in stuccoed stonework whose carved motifs were sharply outlined against the sky along the roof-line. This interplay of symbolic merlons, which were over 3 meters high, lightened the somewhat massive appearance of the Tulunid building.

The Arrival of the Fatimid Caliphs

In the tenth century, the disintegration of the Abbasid empire gathered speed. After ibn Tulun had seceded from the caliphs of Baghdad, the Shiite Buyid princes put the caliphs (who were Sunni Muslims) under their protection. These Persian soldiers of fortune, who became independent in 932, were able to occupy Baghdad, where they intensified Persian influence at the court. From then onwards, the quarrel between the Sunnis and the Shiites, over the succession of the leader of Islam, worsened. The Shiite branch supported the successors of the Prophet's family and considered Ali, the Prophet's cousin and son-in-law (husband of Fatima, the Prophet's daughter), to be the legal representative of the tradition. According to them, the descendants of Muhammad were the only ones who could inherit power and become Guardians of the Islamic faith. This political-religious movement grew rapidly as the Sunni power of Baghdad weakened. In North Africa and the Near East, the Alids were represented by Fatimid anti-caliphs, who constituted the fiercest opposition to Sunnism. The Fatimids, or supporters of Fatima, the Prophet's daughter, formed an Ismaili Shiite dynasty which held sway thanks to Ubaidallah (862–934), who took the title of *mahdi* ("the Rightly-Guided One").

A generous space
Seen from the top of the minaret, the vast courtyard of Ibn Tulun's Great Mosque in Fustat, bordered with wide arcades, surrounds the central fountain used for ritual ablutions. The monument is made of brick, inspired by the creations in Samarra.

Perspective on an arcade
The haughty grandeur of the porticoes bordering the courtyard of Ibn Tulun's Great Mosque, created by a strictly uniform array of sober, single-level arches.

Page 146
The minaret and fountain
In the center of the courtyard of Ibn Tulun's Great Mosque is a dome-covered fountain – a medieval restoration dating from the era of the Mamluks in Cairo (1296). As for the spiral minaret in the background, it is a late reconstruction in stone of an earlier brick building.

Ubaidallah, who passed for a direct descendant of the Prophet, was born in Syria; he fled from his adversaries to Tafilalt in southern Morocco. His missionary, Abu Abd Allah, spread his ideas in Ifriqiya (present-day Tunisia), where he was quickly recognized as the true *mahdi*. His faithful gave him the title of caliph; and from then on there existed, in opposition to the Sunni caliphate in Baghdad, a Shiite caliphate, which first established its authority in Kairouan, the capital of Ifriqiya. Later, in 921, Ubaidallah founded the city of Mahdiya, where he established his new capital.

At the time of the Fatimid dynasty, the Alid movement spread rapidly, establishing itself in Egypt in 969 and in Damascus in 970. Most of the Islamic world seemed at that time ready to come over to the Shiite camp, while Sunnism did not regain its predominant position until it made new converts among the Seljuk Turks. Not only did Turkish soldiers act as guards for the Abbasids, but their brothers, the Seljuks, soon became a formidable power in the Middle East, where they took over Persia before entering Baghdad in triumph in 1055, calling themselves "defenders of the caliph".

The Fatimids brought about profound changes in Egypt. The Shiite caliphs founded Cairo (al-Qahira, "the Victorious"), and established themselves in the new capital in 973. During their reign, Egypt enjoyed extraordinary prosperity, with a revival of the arts and architecture.

General Jawhar, the commander of the troops of the Fatimid al-Muizz (953–975), decided to build this new city, situated between the Nile and the Muqattam Hills, not far from the Arab city of Fustat. It was essentially a fortress, a sort of "forbidden city" reserved for the sovereign and his court, his administrative personnel and his Praetorian Guard. The walled city contained the treasury, the mint, the library, an arsenal and mausoleums. It was built to a square plan, and had a surrounding brick wall, each side measuring 1.1 kilometers. In the eleventh century, on the eve of the Crusades, these walls were rebuilt in stone because of advances in the art of siege laying.

Wide porticoes
The breadth of the large arcades supporting a wood-framed ceiling, the pointed arches supported by pillars with imbedded corner columns, and the endless repetition of the same sober, decorative elements – all are striking features of ibn Tulun's Great Mosque.

Strength and sobriety of the Tulunid style
An arcade facing the courtyard of ibn Tulun's Great Mosque in Cairo. Pointed and slightly horseshoe-shaped arches on rectangular pillars appear in the spandrels, thus lightening the bays. On either side of these openings are large stucco rosettes – a motif also found on a frieze which runs along the top of the wall, recalling the decoration of the mosques in Samarra.

Grandeur and delicacy
Detail of screened (*claustra*) windows made of stucco and decorated with geometric tracery which open on to the *ziyada*, or exterior courtyard. Repeated decorative motifs are frequently used in Islamic houses of prayer.

The nature of Cairo – a fortress where only the ruling class resided – explains in part the profound division which long existed between the Fatimid sovereigns with their court and administration on the one hand, and the great masses of Egyptian laborers, rural and skilled, who remained Sunni, on the other. This social breach accounts for the relative brevity of the Fatimid interlude: the dynasty lasted for only 200 years, ending in chaos in 1171.

The al-Azhar Mosque: A Center of Civilization

Founded in 970, the principal mosque of Shiite Islam for North Africa and the Near East was built between the tenth and twelfth centuries in the center of Cairo. It was called al-Azhar, "the Splendid". The building had an oblong courtyard surrounded by a portico made of reused ancient columns supporting arcades in stuccoed brick. Reused shafts and capitals supported pointed, four-centered brick arches. The design of these bays was remarkably energetic: the arches were raised high and joined to each other by tie rods which lent solidity to the portico, despite the slenderness of its supports. To guard against any risk of weakness, the architects tripled the columns on either side of the entrance and doubled them at the corners of the courtyard. This courtyard measured 50 by 34 meters; its four "façades" were decorated, at the level of the friezes, with recesses directly above the columns. Large circular rosettes were placed above the arches. Set against the sky was a large openwork balustrade with staggered merlons (a theme of Achaemenid origin) which lightened the general appearance of the building. The decorative style used in the courtyard of al-Azhar came, in large measure, from the Tulunid example. Thus, in its ornamentation and its use of brick, the first Fatimid architecture of Cairo conformed to the Mesopotamian tradition brought to Egypt by ibn Tulun – while the reuse of ancient building materials recalled the Umayyad techniques.

In al-Azhar Mosque, the courtyard formed a perfect prologue to the prayer hall, which originally had five bays parallel to the *qibla*. It was a hypostyle with a flat, wooden ceiling supported by reused columns, recalling the structure of the venerable Amr Mosque. There is the same spatial lightness, in which the crisscrossing tie rods create a rhythm at the level of the imposts. This hall offered the novelty of a larger, central basilical nave, bordered by two arcades leading to the

An Islamic university
The al-Azhar Mosque, founded in 970 by the Shiite Fatimids in Cairo, or al-Qahira, which became the Fatimid capital in 973. The mosque's portico opening on to the courtyard is lightened by slender columns supporting pointed arches; the minaret was added in the reign of the Mamluks. At first, al-Azhar was the Shiite university for the whole of the medieval Near East. Later, after the fall of the Fatimid dynasty, it became the center of Sunni doctrine.

mihrab and was underscored by two pairs of columns. Furthermore, the space continued laterally, at right-angles to the sides of the courtyard. It included, to right and left, eleven bays, each three arches wide, which visibly increased the size of the prayer hall. The courtyard gave the impression of being within the *haram* rather than preceding it, thereby lending cohesiveness and unity to the structure.

After the fall of the Fatimids, this Shiite mosque became the great university of Sunni Islam. It underwent several enlargements: the *qibla* was demolished, while the original *mihrab* was preserved and the prayer hall was lengthened, in the direction of Mecca, with four new bays. The principal nave of the new part led to a new *mihrab* which was off-center. To the north, the façade of the entrance was completely remodeled, and Mamluk minarets were added.

The Fatimids created a series of places for prayer, which were used by the anti-caliphs to assert their authority. If al-Muizz and al-Aziz showed tolerance towards the Coptic (Christian) minority, Caliph al-Hakim (996–1021) instigated persecutions of Christians and Jews. This Alid caliph, who prescribed rigorous asceticism, had a vast mosque built to the north of Cairo, which was inspired by the Mosque of ibn Tulun. It consisted of five bays parallel to the *qibla*, with an axial nave leading to the *mihrab*. A triple portico surrounded the courtyard, while the arcades were repeated at the entrance. The building was constructed entirely in brick, with huge pillars supporting pointed arches. On both sides of the main entrance were heavily fortified corner towers whose walls receded towards the top; these were crowned with minarets. The north-east side of the building is part of the Fatimid city wall.

This mosque, which measures 120 by 113 meters, has been ruined by absurd and misguided "restoration" projects. Today it has a paved floor and interior walls of white marble which bear no relation to the original building.

The Stone Walls of Cairo

During the reign of the Fatimid caliph, al-Mustansir (1036–1094), who managed to keep his throne for more than fifty years without ever really ruling, disorder and anarchy prevailed in Egypt. In 1074, in an attempt to restore order to an Egypt in ruins, al-Mustansir appealed to Badr al-Gamali, an Armenian who had been governor of Damascus and prefect of St John of Acre. Badr was protected by Armenian troops who had taken refuge in Egypt three years after their defeat by the Seljuk Turks (1071) in Mantzikert. He immediately confined the caliph to the royal palace. The soldiers, on whom he relied for his authority, were accompanied by architects and engineers who were specialists in fortifications. To them Badr entrusted the task of building a new stone wall around the capital to replace Jawhar's mud-brick wall. Between 1087 and 1091, these builders, working in the

The result of many additions
Plan of the al-Azhar Mosque in Cairo. Several enlargements have been grafted on to the structure with its original courtyard – in particular, new bays at the end of the prayer hall, with a new *mihrab*. As in ibn Tulun's Great Mosque, the porticoes run parallel to the *qibla*.
1. Entrance
2. Porticoed courtyard
3. First prayer hall
4. Additions

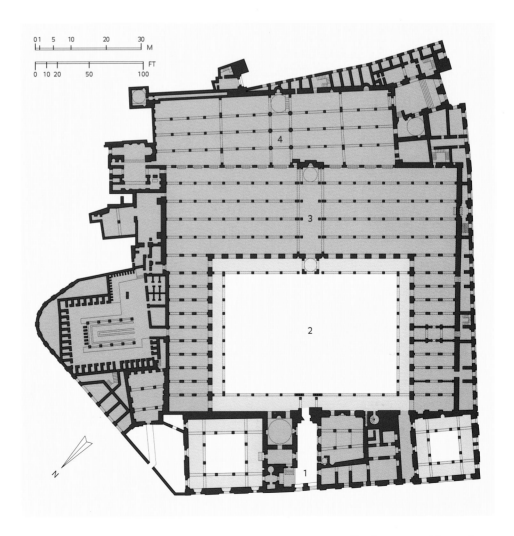

The courtyard portico
With its large medallions over
the arches and its false bays
adorning the spandrels, the courtyard façade of the al-Azhar
Mosque carries on the technique
of stuccoed brick found at the
ibn Tulun Mosque – though the
use of marble columns adds elegance to the structure.

An elegant hypostyle
The arcades of the prayer hall
of al-Azhar are parallel to the
qibla – unlike the porticoes of the
Amr Mosque, whose arcades
are perpendicular. But in both
mosques, tie rods linking the
imposts strengthen the
delicate structures which are
covered by flat, wooden roofs.

The mosque of the mad caliph
This mosque, built in Cairo at the dawn of the eleventh century by the Fatimid caliph, al-Hakim, was visibly influenced by ibn Tulun's Great Mosque. It has powerful corner towers with sloping sides like a fortress. On the upper terrace stands an octagonal minaret, with a small, ribbed dome.

Armenian and Byzantine tradition, constructed the outer walls and curtain walls which were marked by square towers, as well as the gates of Cairo called Bab al-Nasr, Bab al-Futuh and Bab al-Zuwayla. The construction of this exceptionally fine city wall, which was similar to that of Edessa from where a number of Badr's workers came, marked the return of the use of ashlar in Egyptian architecture, thus renewing links with the distant past of the pharaohs. The structure was made of large stone blocks jointed together with extreme precision.

The concept of this wall derived from Roman models, with square or semicircular towers and gates, semicircular arches, and advanced forms such as the groined vault or the cupola set on pendentives. The system of machicolations, inherited from the Umayyad castles, demonstrates the state-of-the-art defenses in Cairo on the eve of the Crusades. This prestigious construction, which still stands today in all its geometric and functional perfection, is an example of the techniques which were later used during the Ayyubid period. It anticipated the great citadels of Damascus and Aleppo.

Pointed arches on brick pillars
Like the ibn Tulun Mosque, al-Hakim's mosque has large brick pillars with embedded corner columns supporting pointed arches. Unfortunately it has recently been radically "restored" leaving only white marble visible instead of the thousand-year-old structures of the Fatimid building, recorded in these photographs.

A New Type of Stone Mosque

The art of stonecutting for defensive structures was also essential to the new mosques which the Fatimid caliphs erected in Cairo. These were not huge edifices, like the congregational buildings described above; nevertheless, this stone architecture produced some remarkable designs. Under the influence of Syrian-Armenian builders of Christian origin, the mosques adopted longitudinal proportions undeniably inherited from the basilical form.

During the reign of Caliph al-Amir (1101–1130) the small mosque of al-Aqmar was built (in 1125). Its longitudinal plan is not more than 30 meters deep by 20 meters wide. The façade facing the street was not parallel to the *qibla*, and this adjustment was achieved by means of a gate placed on a slant, which compensated for the misalignment, following a formula subsequently much used in Mamluk art. The originality of the sculpted decoration of this façade lies in the transposition into stone of decorative motifs which had appeared at al-Azhar, where they were in stuccoed brickwork. Small stalactiform niches, or *muqarnas*, made their first appearance there. Inside, a small, square courtyard surrounded by

An Armenian-Byzantine wall
The city wall given by the vizier Badr al-Gamali to Cairo in 1087 was built by Armenians, heirs to Roman-Byzantine techniques. This engraving shows the door of Bab al-Nasr, as drawn by Louis Mayer in 1802.

Page 158
Saved from disaster
One of the few parts of the al-Hakim Mosque to have escaped the recent drastic renovation is the beautiful *mihrab* with its polychrome marble decoration. Its arch stones use the *ablaq* style, alternating light and dark stones.

a single row of arcades preceded the prayer hall, with its three bays and five naves. The supports are ancient reused columns.

Another Fatimid building based on a rigorously rectangular pattern, that of the mosque of al-Salih Talai, was erected in 1160. The building, around 50 meters long, stood on a podium, access being by means of a double stairway along the façade. The entrance had a recess in the form of a large, exedra set back, supported by a row of four columns. On the main axis, a gate opened on to a courtyard measuring 23 by 18 meters. It was surrounded by a portico with a single row of columns, with six supports running widthwise and seven lengthwise. The prayer hall, as at al-Aqmar, had only three bays parallel to the *qibla*. Al-Salih Talai's coherent and rational system used the architectural language which had been introduced by the Syrian-Armenian builders, under the direction of Badr al-Gamali, less than a century before.

The Palace of the Fatimid Caliphs

The Fatimid period in Egypt saw a remarkable flowering of the arts and sciences. The caliphs promoted artistic expression and employed astronomers, astrologers, mathematicians and scholars who all worked at the court. The ban on making representational images applied only to religion and did not affect scientific and literary works – so the caliphs also employed copyists and illustrators who made miniatures.

On Cairo's main thoroughfare, the sovereign had two large palaces and a

Square towers and curtain walls
The Fatimid walls around Cairo were built between 1087 and 1091, using cut stone dressed in the ancient manner.
Above: Square towers of the Bab al-Nasr Gate.
Below: Crenelated bastions punctuate the straight curtain walls.

square (*maydan*) where polo, imported from the eastern borders of Persia, was played. As Oleg Grabar writes: "[The capital] had become one of the largest and most cosmopolitan urban complexes of the medieval world" (Grabar, p. 172). We know about the Great Eastern Palace from contemporary historical accounts which describe the appearance of the rooms leading to the *aula regia*. It is easy to imagine the pomp displayed by the Fatimids in these buildings. Indeed, influenced by Persian courtly ritual, the pre-eminence of the sovereign had become considerable, to the point where al-Hakim wished to have himself acknowledged as a god. Despite the egalitarian character of Muslim doctrine, the deification of princes, following the Roman example, threatened to reappear under the influence of the Shiites.

The Fatimid Mausoleums of Aswan

In southern Egypt, not far from the city of Aswan, lies a necropolis whose mausoleums with partially ruined cupolas bear witness to the development of funerary brick architecture at the time of the Fatimids (eleventh century). The interest of these monuments, or *qubbat*, lies in the variety of domes which covered the tombs and which, in the Islamic world, often symbolize the sky. There are hemi-

The dawn of the First Crusade
Cairo's stone wall was completed four years before Pope Urban II's call to arms for the First Crusade (1095); twenty years previously, the invasion of the Seljuks had spread panic throughout the Near East. The Fatimid capital was defended by the Roman-style gates, with semicircular towers, of Bab al-Futuh (right) and Bab al-Zuwayla (left) – the latter topped with minarets built by the Mamluk al-Mu'ayyad in about 1415.

A return to stone mosques
The influence of the Armenian-Byzantine builders of Badr al-Gamali led to the abandonment of brick for houses of prayer. The small al-Aqmar Mosque (1125) shows this stylistic change: its façade is decorated with motifs – tympanum, stalactites and niches with small columns – transposed into dressed stone.

The entrance portico
In the middle of the building's narrow façade, the entrance hall of the al-Salih Talai Mosque opens behind a row of columns supporting an arcade. The vocabulary of this stone architecture has completely changed: In a very austere style, it is now looser and more refined.

Arcades with tie-rods

The courtyard of the al-Salih Talai Mosque, constructed in 1160, is very light: the porticoes have wooden tie rods connecting the imposts.

A smaller scale

The era of vast prayer halls – like those in the mosques of ibn Tulun, al-Azhar or al-Hakim – was over. The al-Salih Talai Mosque in Cairo had a very sober rectangular plan. The small courtyard is bordered with a portico of raised arches supported by slender columns.

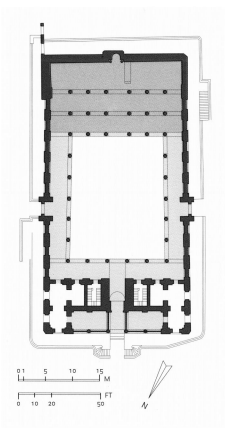

spherical cupolas, some ribbed, some placed on drums with projecting cornices lit by windows. A whole repertoire of styles is tried out here, from the square plan to the cylinder, by way of stalactites which adorn the pendentives with their geometric structures.

This virtuosity of hemispherical forms, and the treatment of the spatial transition from the square to the circle using purely rational forms, marks the first steps in a process that was to fuel the medieval architectural language of Persia and Syria as well as Egypt, and thence the whole area under Islamic influence from Granada to India.

Raised arches
The al-Salih Talai Mosque in Cairo has pointed arches with a double focal point – with close breastwork and steeper pitches – which rise above the capitals. Despite the importance of dressed stone, the stucco decoration of the first Fatimid buildings is still used here.

The Fatimid tombs of Aswan
The Aswan cemetery, in southern
Egypt, has a series of Shiite
mausoleums with brick cupolas
faced with stucco, dating from the
eleventh and twelfth centuries. In
these tombs are many variations
on the form of the dome – ribbed,
raised, on a drum, in quarters,
etc. – which make the *qubba* a
treasury of original designs.

The Disintegration of the Far Western Empire

From Aghlabid Ifriqiya to the Maghreb of the Almohads

Among the provinces which opposed the Abbasid power of Baghdad, and gradually seceded, was Ifriqiya (modern Tunisia). Though Arab raiders reached northern
Africa by 647, the second expedition did not take place until 665. It was not until
670 that Ifriqiya was annexed and Islamic troops founded the city of Kairouan,
meaning "Encampment". Kairouan was situated in arid desert, 150 kilometers
south of Tunis and 60 kilometers west of Susah (modern Sousse). In 836, a Great
Mosque was built there, making Kairouan the fourth holy city of Sunni Islam.

However, the Arab conquest was not easily accomplished: there was stiff resistance from the Byzantines, and especially from the Berbers. The Muslim general,
Uqba ibn Nafi, was defeated at Biskra (in present-day Algeria) in 682. Kusayla,
leader of the Berber insurrection, was able to put the Arab invaders to flight, and
they had to undertake a new expedition in order to seize Carthage in 698. The
resistance was led by a Berber queen, al-Kahina, who held off the Muslims,
becoming a legend in the Aurès Mountains (in present-day Algeria). Her defeat in
702 led to the "Arabization" of the country, and of a large part of the Maghreb,
under a governor who was dependent on the Umayyads of Damascus.

It was by recruiting the Berbers, whose lifestyle was similar to that of the
inhabitants of Arabia, that the Muslim forces were able to achieve brilliant victories. An army led by Tariq landed in Spain in 711. The Arab who relieved him, Musa
ibn Nusayr, brought the new province into the Umayyad camp. But these Berbers,
who imposed taxes on their non-Arabic subjects, affirmed their independence by
embracing the eastern Kharijite heresy (a doctrine which proclaimed the equality
of all Muslims). The followers of this strictly communal sect seized Kairouan in
745, just before the fall of the Umayyads. There followed a period of uncertainty,
during which the reins of power slipped from the orthodox Sunnis.

Under the Aghlabid dynasty, which lasted from 800 to 909 in the eastern part
of North Africa, religious orthodoxy was restored in a province which was to continue to be semi-independent. Ibrahim ibn al-Aghlab, named emir by Baghdad,
was responsible for this return to stability. At his castle, called Kasr al-Khedim,
near Kairouan, he had a praetorian guard of black slaves. From this base he began a vigorous campaign to regain power. His successor, Ziyadatallah I, launched
expeditions against Sicily, which he managed to conquer in 827. It was he who
built the minaret of the Great Mosque of Kairouan in 836.

Kairouan and Its Great Mosque

The Great Mosque of Kairouan was built in several stages, in 836, 862 and 875.
The building, which covered an area of 130 by 80 meters (about 2.5 acres or
1 hectare), was surrounded by a high, fortified wall in which there were eight
gates. There was a courtyard 65 meters long by 50 meters wide, surrounded by
double porticoes. The whole was dominated by a tan, square minaret of three stories, each one narrower than the one below. This type of minaret seems to have
been derived from ancient sea-marks, and is reminiscent of the Lighthouse of

Alexandria, images of which are found on coins. It spread throughout the Maghreb and Spain, from the Kutubiyya Mosque in Marrakesh to the Giralda Tower of the Great Mosque of Seville.

The oblong prayer hall was composed of seventeen naves with arcades perpendicular to the *qibla*. The wider central nave led to the *mihrab*, following a formula which al-Azhar was to use again in Cairo. Of the eight bays, the last one alongside the *qibla* was also accentuated. In the center, a cupola dominated the niche; this indicated the direction for prayer – a typical plan for a mosque in the form of a "T". This was a hypostyle building in which ancient elements, both columns and capitals, were reused. The *haram*, with its central nave bordered with twin columns, had 160 columns in all. Like the Amr Mosque in Cairo, the arcades were joined by ties at the level of the imposts. They supported a flat wood-framed ceiling.

The decoration of the *mihrab* is of great interest. It was made of 130 faïence tiles with metallic highlights, imported from Baghdad. The niche itself was formed by marble panels some of which were perforated. Finally, the *minbar*, in teak with the same motifs in finely worked tracery, dates from the reign of Ibrahim ibn al-Aghlab, at the beginning of the ninth century. A ribbed cupola rose above the *mihrab*. It stood on an octagon supported by four pendentives, alternating with arches of the same size, forming the transition from the square plan to the circle. Another cupola, in the middle of the south-east gate of the courtyard, marked the axial entrance to the prayer hall.

Outside the city walls of Kairouan, huge circular tanks were used as reservoirs to provide water for the city. The largest, measuring 128 meters in diameter, was built by Abu Ibrahim Ahmad in 860. These cisterns were the culmination of a remarkable water system: built of stone walls, they were reinforced by luttressed semicircular structures designed to resist the pressure of the water. The cisterns were fed by an aqueduct 36 kilometers long, leading from the Marguelil Wadi. The main pool, preceded by a small settling tank 37 meters in diameter, had a small

Page 171

The Aghlabid minaret
The square minaret of the Great Mosque in Kairouan: its three massive levels are topped with a ribbed dome, creating a powerful silhouette which influenced all North African and Andalusian architecture.

The Great Mosque of Kairouan
The Aghlabid mosque of Kairouan, viewed from the top of the minaret, showing the courtyard and the *haram*. Constructed in 836, the Great Mosque is the most venerable house of prayer in the Maghreb.

island in the center where, it was said, "the emir used to relax". If this were indeed true, it would be a re-creation of the small island in the middle of a circular pool which the Roman writer Varro described, when speaking of his "aviary", and which copied Hadrian's "Maritime Theater" in Tivoli. Both these constructions were connected with courtly ritual and the use of horoscopes common in the Hellenistic and Roman courts, from which we know the Muslim sultans drew inspiration. Thus the Aghlabid dynasty in Kairouan continued to perpetuate the palace liturgy of antiquity – as did the courts of Cordoba, Baghdad and Cairo.

The Mosque and Ribat of Susah

Like Kairouan, Susah (the ancient city of Hadrumetum) owed its renaissance to the Aghlabids. From this Mediterranean port, dating back to Phoenician and Roman times, Islamic forces embarked to conquer Sicily. Its Great Mosque, located in the center of the city, was built in 851, at the same time as the Great Mosque in Kairouan. It owes its squat, powerful appearance to its origin as an ancient *kasbah*, or fortress, for the defense of the harbor. Transformed into a place of prayer, this building retained its corner towers and merlons. The oblong courtyard, with its stocky pillars and heavy arcades of horseshoe arches, led to the *haram* which, as in Kairouan, had an axial cupola over the portico leading to the prayer hall, and another cupola over the *mihrab*. Of the eleven naves, with arcades perpendicular to the *qibla* and stonework vaults overhead, only the wider central nave is emphasized. Its beautiful horseshoe arches stood on square pillars, sometimes flanked by reused columns.

The *ribat* (or monastic fort) next to the Great Mosque of Susah was built at the end of the eighth century to guard the entry to the port and repel the Byzantine

Ribbed dome
An octagonal dome with wide ribs soars above the *mihrab*, marking the most sacred spot of the Mosque of Kairouan. The transition from the square plan to the circle can clearly be seen in the intermediate phase of the octagon, with slightly concave ribs.

Page 173
The scale of the hypostyle hall
The prayer hall of Kairouan, its reused antique and Byzantine columns supporting the seventeen arcades perpendicular to the *qibla*.

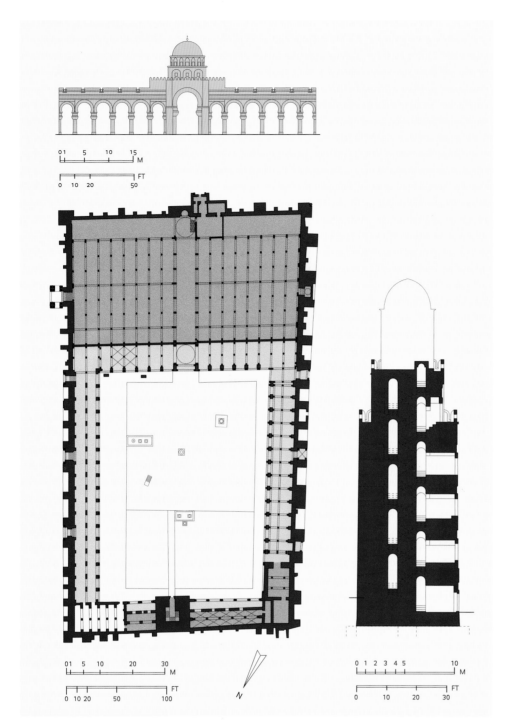

The Great Mosque of the Aghlabids
Elevation of the courtyard façade, plan and cross-section of the minaret. The prayer hall has seventeen naves. The central nave is larger, as is the last bay, and both are accentuated, giving rise to the T-shaped plan, which was common in the Maghreb. The 35-meter minaret has six stories with inclined planes.

naval forces which were still masters of the Mediterranean. The *ribat* was a square fortress, with walls surmounted with merlons, dominated by a high, round tower, built in 821 by the Aghlabid emir Ziyadatallah I. A similar *ribat*, built in 796 for the warriors of the Muslim faith, stood by the sea in Monastir, but it is now much less well-preserved than the Ribat of Susah. Though it underwent numerous additions from the ninth to the eleventh centuries, it never lost its proud, massive character, making it a remarkable example of Islamic military architecture in the classical period.

The structure beneath the dome
One of the doors of the Great
Mosque of Kairouan is marked by
a dome which is supported by four
slightly horseshoe-shaped arches.

Access to the holy of holies
Opposite: The *mihrab* of the Great
Mosque of Kairouan is one of the
most famous in the Islamic world.
Surrounded by decorative ceramic
tiles from Mesopotamia, it has
a niche with perforated marble
panels. The two marble columns at
the sides have Byzantine capitals.
Above: Detail of the decoration of
the *minbar* of Kairouan, with its
perforated *claustra* motifs carved
in wood.

Large waterworks
Outside the walls of Kairouan, the Aghlabid tanks are huge, circular reservoirs where drinking water, brought by aqueduct, was stored to meet the needs of the city's population.

The Fortress-Mosque of Susah
View from the top of the keep
of the Susah Ribat. The mosque
was built in 851 under the
Aghlabids, the result of refitting
an ancient *kasbah* used for fighting
the Byzantines who had tried to
regain a foothold in North Africa.

A powerful *haram*
The prayer hall of the mosque in
Susah, with its low supports
and raised arches has a massive
appearance, indicative of the
insecurity at large when it was
being built.

Militant architecture
The mosque in Susah preserves the squat forms of its warrior origins, with arcades of depressed arches, and steps leading to the parapet walks and fortified corner towers.

The *castrum* or Roman military formula
Plan of the Ribat or fortress-mosque of Susah, organized as a square Roman camp. Its surrounding walls, punctuated by towers, give it a markedly military character. Around the porticoes of the courtyard were the cells of the warrior-monks.

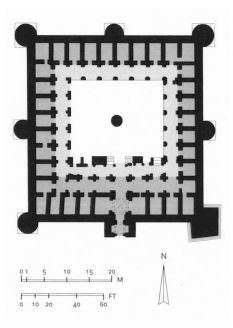

Page 179
The watch-tower
The Ribat of Susah dominated the port city. To prevent any Byzantine incursion, watchmen surveyed the seaward approaches from the top of the high, cylindrical tower which rises from the crenelated walls.

A *patio* of light
The open-air courtyard of the Aljaferiya Palace in Saragossa is bordered by wide multifoil arches, giving an impression of great levity.

Delicacy of the *claustra*
The bays of this twin window in the Aljaferiya Palace are topped with horse-shoe arches, and covered with screens of fine open-work which filter the light.

The Almoravids and Almohads of Spain and the Maghreb

In 1061, the Almoravid dynasty founded its capital in Marrakesh (in present-day Morocco). These sovereigns came to Spain at the request of the emir of Seville. They launched the second Islamic invasion of the Iberian peninsula, soon followed by that of the Almohads.

Both the stricter Almoravids – who absolutely rejected any motif that was not abstract and geometrical – and the Almohads (who succeeded them from 1147 to 1269) envisioned a renewal of Islam. Like the Almoravids, the Almohads were Berbers from North Africa. They followed the doctrine of Muhammad ibn Tumart, who called himself the *mahdi* who had come to purify Islam and begin a reign of justice and true faith. Their name (taken from the Arabic *al-muwahhidun*) denoted the "unitarian" movements which emphasized the unity of Allah. Ibn Tumart's comrade, Abd al-Mumin (1128-1163), took the title of caliph and reigned in North Africa and Andalusia. In 1150, he founded the city of Rabat (*al-Ribat*), which became the capital of his kingdom. Under the Almohads a sober, severe art flourished, reflecting the asceticism the caliph wished to promote.

Page 187

The Synagogue of Toledo
Known as Santa Maria la Blanca, this synagogue was built between 1075 and 1085 by Moorish artisans experienced in Arab forms: horseshoe arches, porticoes perpendicular to the end wall, floral and geometrical decoration, etc. This beautiful space, consecrated to Judaism, is covered by a wood-framed ceiling. In observance of the Second Commandment, Jewish-Arabic artistry has adopted a pine-cone motif as capital adornment.

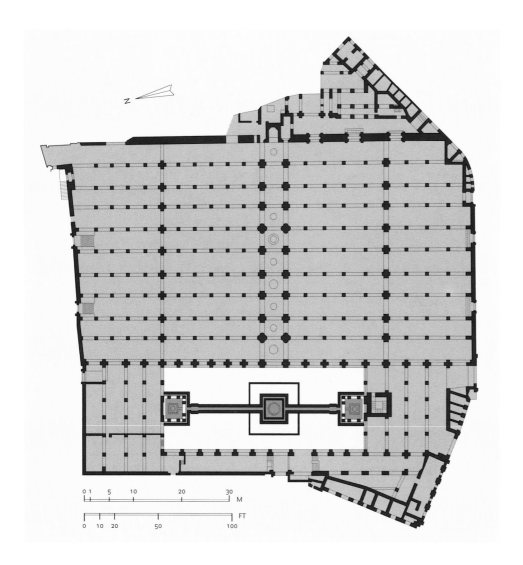

Plan of the Qarawiyin Mosque
in present-day Morocco,
constructed mainly at the time of
the Almoravids (1135). It has an
oblong courtyard with ablution
pools. Its prayer hall has multiple
bays whose arcades are parallel
to the *qibla*. The irregular shape
of the building results from its
successive stages of growth and
its location in a densely populated
area.

The construction methods and general style of the eleventh- and twelfth-century buildings consisted of hypostyle mosques with their horseshoe or multi-foil arches, square or cruciform pillars and sober arcades perpendicular to the *qibla*; they also tended to have a T-shaped plan. These elements affected all religious architecture. Similarly, following the distant model of the minaret of Kairouan, the larger mosques had high, square towers, often without any decorative top, whose façades were decorated with tracery carved in geometric designs, offset by intertwined arches on small columns which defined the windows of each story.

The sharply pointed arches, often multifoil or scalloped, the play of stalactite arches (or *muqarnas*) of eastern origin, and the fortress-like character of the places of prayer occasioned by the political disturbances of the Middle Ages – all these elements combine to make Hispano-Moorish art a coherent system which spread throughout the Maghreb and southern Spain.

This type of mosque – with its classical architectural plan – illustrates the desire of the Almoravids and Almohads to establish links with Islam's traditional past. This is embodied in the Great Mosque of Algiers, built in 1097, which had eleven naves and a small oblong courtyard. The Qarawiyin Mosque of Fez, founded in 857 and rebuilt in 912, 933 and 1135, finally covered an area of 6,000 square meters with more than 200 columns. It had ten bays, with arcades parallel to the *qibla*. This is surprising given that Qarawiyin means "from Kairouan", named in memory of its founder, a certain Fatima who fled Tunisia with a group of followers hostile to the Fatimids. The plan of the Qarawiyin Mosque in fact had nothing in common with that of the prayer hall at Kairouan. Like the al-Azhar Mosque in

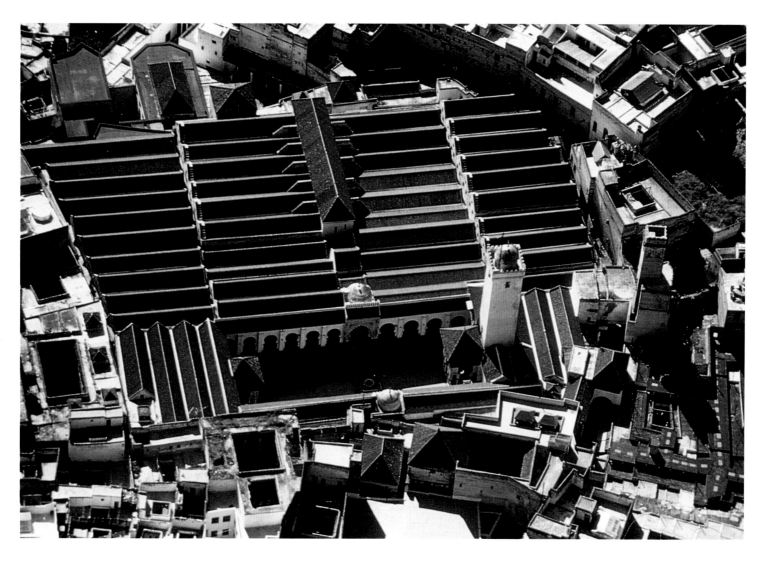

Continual enlargement
Aerial view showing the attempts, between 857 and 1613, to adapt the Qarawiyin Mosque in Fez to the needs of the faithful in this city of the Maghreb.

Massive power
The prayer hall of the Qarawiyin Mosque, whose arcades rest on squat pillars. In this tangle of powerful arches, the space takes on a maze-like appearance.

Towers and minarets

Heirs of the powerful square minaret of Kairouan, the minaret of the Great Mosque of Seville (called the Giralda Tower) and that of the Kutubiyya Mosque of Marrakesh emphasize the asceticism of the Almohads and the Almoravids, with their pure forms and simple decorative style, limited to simple repeated motifs. Note that the upper stories of the Giralda Tower are additions made when the minaret was converted into a cathedral bell tower.

Sentinel on the Guadalquivir River

Watching over the river, the Tower of Gold in Seville is a twelve-sided building built by Abu Yaqub Yusuf in the twelfth century.

Page 191
The Kutubiyya Mosque in Marrakesh

The beautiful internal space of the "Mosque of the Bookshops" combines bare, slightly pointed horseshoe arches with long perspectives – creating an ascetic effect typical of twelfth-century Almohad art.

A mausoleum with stalactites
One of the most interesting tombs of Marrakesh is the Almoravid Qubba Barudiyin, with its fine network of delicately worked *muqarnas* which alternate with scallop shells.

Octogonal cupola
View of the roof with stalactites over the funeral chamber of the Qubba Baruadiyin, with its fine array of delicately worked *muqar-nas* alternating with scallop shells.

A sophisticated plan
The Qubba Baruadiyin in Marrakesh is an interesting example of the successive adaptations of the octagonal plan, developed to the highest level in the Great Mosque of Cordoba. The octagonal roof is formed by two squares set at 45° angles to each other.

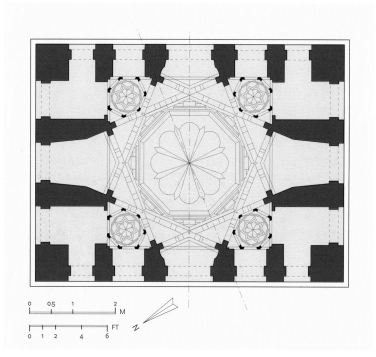

Cairo, this building had an oblong courtyard, flanked on either side by bays linked to the hypostyle – meaning that the courtyard must have been included in the *haram* (a frequent feature of Arab-Andalusian architecture). A lovely ablution pool embellished the open space, at either end of which were pavilions on small columns, supporting a pyramidal roof. These additions date from 1613 and were inspired by the Court of Lions of the Alhambra Palace of Granada.

The beginning of Almohad architecture is epitomized by an example of great purity, the Friday Mosque of Tinmal in the Atlas mountains of Morocco. It was constructed in 1153 by al-Mumin in the place where ibn Tumart began his teaching, and is buried. This unusual building took the form of a fortified *ribat*, a true "Castle of God". It had a square plan, with sides of 50 meters. The prayer hall had nine naves, the central and two lateral ones being accentuated. There was a larger bay in front of the *mihrab*. The building, in stuccoed brick, has recently been beautifully restored, and provides an example of the great conceptual rigor of a strictly symmetrical plan.

The Great Mosque of Seville has today largely disappeared, having been replaced by the Gothic cathedral; only the beautiful minaret, built in 1171, still remains from the original building. The topmost part of the mosque was a later Christian addition of baroque layers, on top of which they placed a bronze angel as a weather-vane, from which it gets its name, the Giralda Tower. The decoration of this minaret influenced that of the Great Mosque of Hassan in Rabat.

One of the most beautiful minarets of western Islam, built between 1157 and 1195, towered over the Kutubiyya, or "Mosque of the Bookshops", in Marrakesh. Contemporary with the Giralda Tower, it rose to a height of 69 meters. Its square plan and rectilinear profile, like a castle keep surmounted by a lantern, provided beautiful surfaces for the decoration of intertwined arches covering the upper sections of its walls. The prayer hall of this vast mosque had seventeen naves and seven bays, 80 meters wide, with a large transept and the typical T-shaped plan of this period.

Compared to the architecture of the Umayyads, this deliberately austere architecture contributed no innovations. Throughout, there are the same plans, the same ribbed cupolas over the *mihrab*, and the same type of ornamentation treated in the same sober fashion. Thus it was an art that faithfully reflected the austerity preached by the theologians of the age of the Almoravid and Almohad sovereigns.

The Ziza Palace in Palermo

In Sicily, conquered by the Aghlabids of Kairouan, the Arabs were supplanted by the Christian king, Roger I of Hauteville, who took Messina in 1061 and Palermo in 1072. Under the Normans, Sicily became the center of a mixed Arab-Christian culture, thanks to the tolerance of Roger II, king of Sicily from 1130 to 1154. The Byzantine and Arab currents intermingled harmoniously. Scientists and poets converged on the city of Palermo, where Europeans could drink at the fountains of ancient knowledge through the intermediary of Arab men of letters. Under William II, successor to Roger II, the equilibrium seemed to hold – but in fact the situation was deteriorating because of the presence of French Catholics who created a crusade-like atmosphere. Persecutions against Muslims led to the death of the king in 1189.

The art of Palermo reveals Arab influences in a series of buildings, among which were the Palatine Chapel (Capella Palatina) and the church of San Cataldo, dating from 1160, with its curious row of cupolas. But it was even more evident in the remarkable Ziza Palace (from al-Aziza, "the Glorious"). Built in 1185, this massive edifice with a high, four-story façade, was entered through an internal transverse portico leading to the state room. This hall, in the form of a sort of open *iwan*, was decorated with Byzantine style mosaics depicting a royal hunting scene on a gold

The Friday Mosque in Tinmal
Built by al-Mumin in 1153, the Almohad mosque in Tinmal is an example of the purity of forms promoted by the Berber dynasties of North Africa. The building is being restored, allowing the visitor to imagine the place where ibn Tumart lived. With its walls crowned with battlements, the building is a "Stronghold of Allah".

background. The mosaics hung above an interior fountain which bubbled beneath a stalactite vault. Its murmuring waters ran the whole length of a sloping area – a device already used in the rotunda of Nero's *Domus Aurea* in Rome.

On the second floor, this Norman-Arab palace repeated the strictly symmetrical plan of the lower level, within a rectangle 40 by 20 meters. In the center of the *piano nobile* was a sumptuous audience chamber with *iwans* on either side. There was another fountain, fed by an ingenious mechanism supplied by an aqueduct. The third floor repeated the same structure, with an empty space above the audience chamber, which was two stories high. This complex plan, with its alcoves and *iwans*, was again repeated on the fourth floor. Most of the ceilings were covered with superb stalactite decorations.

The design adopted at Ziza by the Christian king, using Arab architects and artisans, was inspired by the Zirid Palace in Ashir (in present-day Algeria) – a palace which had crumbled under Norman attack. The Zirid Palace (built, as its name suggests, during the Zirid dynasty) dated from the tenth century, and had a

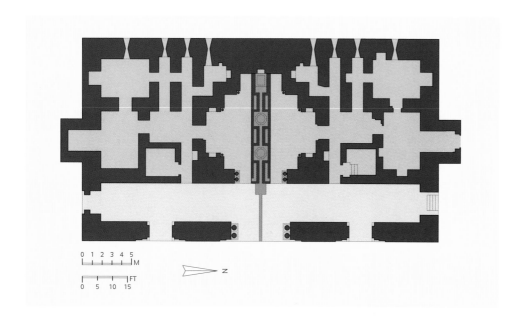

0 1 2 3 4 5 M

0 5 10 15 FT

N

A strictly geometrical plan
Plan of the Ziza Palace in Palermo, Sicily, built in 1185. It follows the tradition of Arab palaces whose symmetrical rectilinear plans date back to the Almoravid era, such as the Castillo of Monteagudo or Murcia. In the center of the *aula regia* (throne room) is a pool with waterspouts, fed by a hydraulic system.

similar symmetrical, rectangular plan – though it was much larger, covering 72 by 40 meters with a central courtyard of 24 by 22 meters, at the end of which there was an *aula regia* in the form of a triple apse.

Except for the mosaics, all of the decoration of King William II's palace in Palermo was derived from Islamic art – an indication of the lively fashion for Islamic artistic and cultural traditions at the end of the twelfth century. At the end of this early era, Arab architecture was a source of inspiration for the synagogues of the Jewish community of Toledo, as well as for the palaces of Norman Christian kings of Sicily. As attested to by the mixed civilizations which flourished in both Sicily and Spain, Islamic art reached its apogee where it converged with western Christendom, on the eve of the fall of the Abbasid caliphate in the mid-thirteenth century.

The Ziza Palace in Palermo
With its austere appearance, the Arab-Norman Ziza Palace in Palermo stands three stories tall, with a massive façade in which there are three doors, arranged hierarchically.

Islam with Byzantium
In the form of an *iwan*, the great niche, which greets the visitor at the entrance of the Ziza Palace in Palermo, combines Byzantine mosaics on a gold background, with Islamic stalactite structures. The figurative motif illustrates the theme of the royal hunt.

Page 196 below
Transverse vestibule
Behind the façade of the Ziza Palace, a vaulted entrance hall leads to the formal state rooms on the upper floors. In the *iwan* which opens in its center, the sovereign gave audiences to his people.

Interplay of stalactites
The characteristic form of the *muqarnas* developed during the late eleventh and early twelfth centuries. These honeycomb structures were later to become an essential element in Islamic decoration.

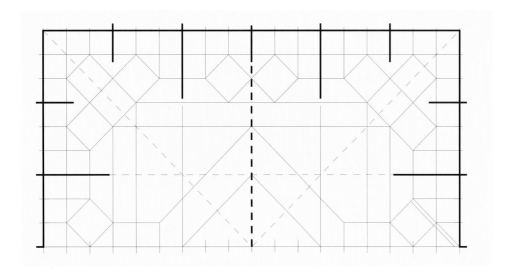

Based on the double square
The plan of the Ziza Palace's stalactite niches derives from the plan of the palace itself, which is also based on the proportion of 1:2.

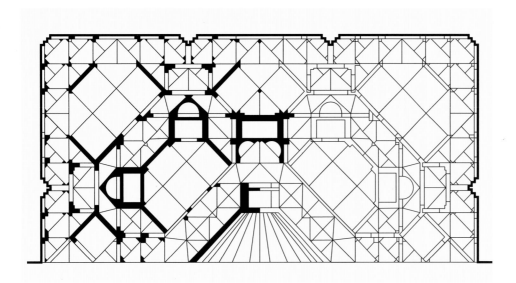

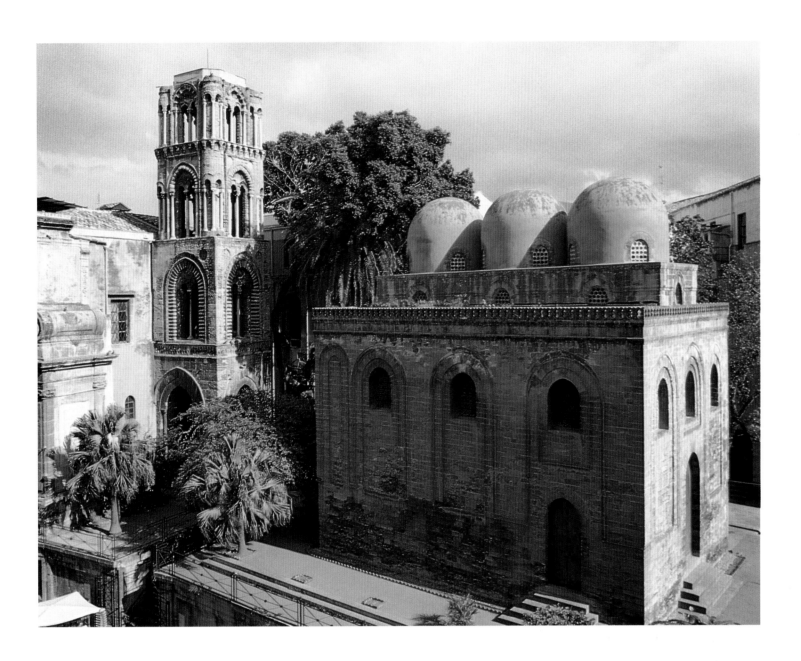

Arab style in Palermo
Dating from 1160, the church of
San Cataldo, in Palermo, with its
tall, red cupolas, shows the
influence of Islamic architecture
in the Norman court.

Upheavals in the Near East

The Rise of the Ayyubids
and the Decline of the Abbasids

The entry of the Seljuks into Jerusalem in 1079 triggered a spate of fighting throughout the Mediterranean. The reaction of European Christians was to launch the Crusades in 1095. These expeditions were conceived both as pilgrimages to the Holy Sepulcher and as holy wars to liberate the Eastern Christians from the Turks. The invasion of Anatolia by the Seljuks, who defeated the Byzantine troops at the battle of Manzikert (1071), not only directly affected the Orthodox Christian communities of Asia Minor, but also overturned a gradually improving *status quo* between Arabs and Christians in Jerusalem. The first Crusade ended in 1099 with the recovery of Jerusalem from the Muslims and the establishment of the Latin Kingdom of Jerusalem which lasted until the fall of Acre in 1291 to the Mamluk troops of al-Ashraf Khalil.

Before the end of the Fatimid dynasty in Cairo, the Crusaders had occupied part of Egypt as a result of the quarrels which erupted at that time over the succession to the caliphate. For a time the Franks even threatened Cairo. It was at this point that Saladin (Salah al-Din, 1171–1193) appeared on the scene. First he served as prefect of Alexandria, then as the prime minister to a Syrian general who opposed the Alid caliph on behalf of Nur al-Din, *atabeg* of Aleppo (1146–1174) and later of Damascus (1154). Saladin, Nur al-Din's nephew, ended the anti-caliphate of Cairo in 1171. The fall of the Fatimids went unnoticed in the subequent violent clashes between Christians and Muslims – but it allowed Saladin to create a new power, uniting Egypt and Syria under the aegis of the Ayyubids in 1183.

Saladin, the son of Ayyub who reigned in the Baalbek region, was of Kurdish origin and a Sunni. Flushed with victories, he demanded that the caliph of Baghdad make him sovereign of Egypt, which included Upper Mesopotamia. He united that territory with Syria in order to form a powerful kingdom to defeat the Franks in the Holy Land. Thanks to Saladin, the Islamic troops were able to defeat the Crusaders at Hattin and enter Jerusalem in 1187. On Saladin's death, the vast territory controlled by the Muslims, which extended as far as Yemen, was divided into several small sultanates.

New Trends in Architecture

The ups and downs of the eleventh and twelfth centuries had two main causes. One was the mix of populations caused by the arrival of Turks from central Asia, with customs which they had inherited from Persia. The other was the Sunni renewal, brought about by these new converts who were strenuously opposed to the Alids.

Under the Seljuks, Aleppo's Great Mosque received a square minaret in ashlar, constructed in 1089 by a local architect named Hasan ibn Mufarraj al-Sarmani. The monument was 46 meters high and 5 meters wide, with five stories decorated with multifoil arches. The cornice at the top, supported by rows of stalactite decorations, or *muqarnas*, had a gallery from which the muezzin summoned the faithful to prayer.

A minaret crowned with stalactites
The minaret of the Great Mosque of Aleppo, built entirely of stone, is topped with *muqarnas*. Constructed in 1089, it marks the sudden arrival of Seljuks in the Mediterranean region.

Beehives cover a cupola

The entrance of the Muristan al-Nuri (or Nur al-Din Hospital) in Damascus dates from 1154. It is covered with a square stone cupola, whose inner surface is covered with geometric stalactites. This work illustrates the virtuosity of Syrian stonecutters.

Later, under Nur al-Din, the stalactite motif was further developed, this covers the cupola of the Muristan (hospital) al-Nuri. Indeed, this wonderful beehive-like building shows a remarkable resourcefulness making it possible for the intrados of the cupolas to be richly decorated, while at the same time reinforcing them.

The Development of Military Architecture

Although Badr al-Gamali had, in 1087, provided Cairo with a strong, defensive stone wall, the invasion of the Seljuks and then the Crusaders caused intense architectural activity in the area of defensive constructions designed to resist sieges. One example was the formidable citadel, begun by Saladin in 1176, to the south of Cairo at the foot of the Muqattam Hills. It was a huge undertaking and a break with tradition, since the fortress stood outside the centers of Fustat and Cairo, on a steeply sloping site dominating the residential areas. It was divided into two parts, each having its own walls: the castle, where the garrison was stationed; and the palace, where the sultan lived. Facing the old city, the fortress had two impressive gates. To the south, towards the mountain, there was a strong wall with semicircular towers which were built, for the most part, after Saladin's reign.

In order to finish the colossal project, Saladin made use of Christian prisoners-of-war, of which there were several thousand, and materials from the pyramids of Giza and the buildings of the pharaohs in the Abusir region. According to an inscription, the first stage of the work ended in 1184. The inscription refers to the fortress with its wall 1,700 meters in circumference, enclosing an area of 32 acres (13 hectares). The fortress incorporated all the military techniques perfected in the confrontation with the Crusaders. The ramparts were 3.5 meters thick, with towers and casemates. The scale of the project was such that, fifty years after Saladin's death, work was still in progress.

In the western part, a second adjacent wall probably enclosed the palace, of which only a few vestiges remain. A huge open area, measuring 600 by 100 meters – called *maydan* in Persian – was the site for official parades and exercises of the sultan's troops, and for games of polo. This Salah al-Din Maydan represents a continuation of the Roman and Byzantine tradition, and exceeds the dimensions both of the *Circus Maximus* of Rome and the great hippodrome of Constantinople.

The Citadels of Damascus and Aleppo

In 1206, thirty years after the start of the work on Saladin's walled citadel in Cairo, a wall was built around the old city of Damascus by Saladin's brother. This was a rectangular enclosure with an east-west orientation, like the *temenos* on which the Great Mosque of the Umayyads had been built nearby. The walls to the north run adjacent to the Barada River, which acts as a moat. The enclosure, around 240 meters long, is punctuated by twelve rectangular towers, constructed

Saladin's hippodrome
At the foot of Cairo's citadel, the sultan of Egypt created a vast open area, the Salah al-Din Maydan, where troops paraded, and polo – a game enjoyed by the Ayyubids, and the Fatimids before them – was played (engraving of Louis Mayer, 1802).

with large rusticated stones. These towers had projecting bartizans topped by machicolations. At the corners, and in the middle of the outer façades, these bartizans were supported by powerful corbels through which the defenders could send missiles. The cantilevered construction supporting a wall protecting the defenders was one of the principal innovations in military architecture during the era of the Crusades. Along its entire circumference, the wall is topped with large merlons pierced with arrow slots in the form of loopholes.

The same techniques were used to build the citadel of Aleppo as that of Damascus – but they were taken to a much higher level. Built on a rise of ground in the shape of a truncated cone, worked by man to form a very steep, paved glacis, Aleppo was one of the most impressive defensive structures in the Near East. For thousands of years this rocky mound had been a refuge for the local inhabitants; soon the entire area was occupied, and the city had nowhere else to expand but the plain. During Hellenistic times, the only buildings left on the summit of the acropolis were the fortifications, the temples and the palace. On the site of the

The Citadel of Damascus
In the heart of the old city of Damascus is the citadel. Built in 1206 by Saladin's brother, it had towers and large rusticated stone, with bartizans containing machicolations. The Crusades produced decisive advances in military architecture.

Roman-Byzantine fortresses, a Muslim fortress was constructed by the Ayyubid Zahir al-Ghazi, son of Saladin, at the end of the twelfth century (and completed in 1209). Later, in 1258, the citadel of Aleppo was destroyed by the Mongols, and then rebuilt in 1292. Destroyed once again, this time by Tamerlane (Timur i Leng), it was restored in the sixteenth century by the Ottomans. Despite all this, the walls and defenses remain essentially as they were during the time of the Ayyubids.

Rising 50 meters above the city of Aleppo, this acropolis has a flattened oval surface 300 meters east to west and 170 meters north to south. Its surrounding wall included forty-two square, projecting towers. Access is on the southern side of the citadel which stood in proud isolation at the top of its glacis. A stout bastion, in the form of a square tower, stood in the middle of the enclosure. To cross the wide surrounding ditch and climb the steep glacis, the architects devised an inclined bridge, supported by seven tall, narrow arches. This bridge linked the barbican at the entrance, which acted as the bridgehead, in the strict sense of the

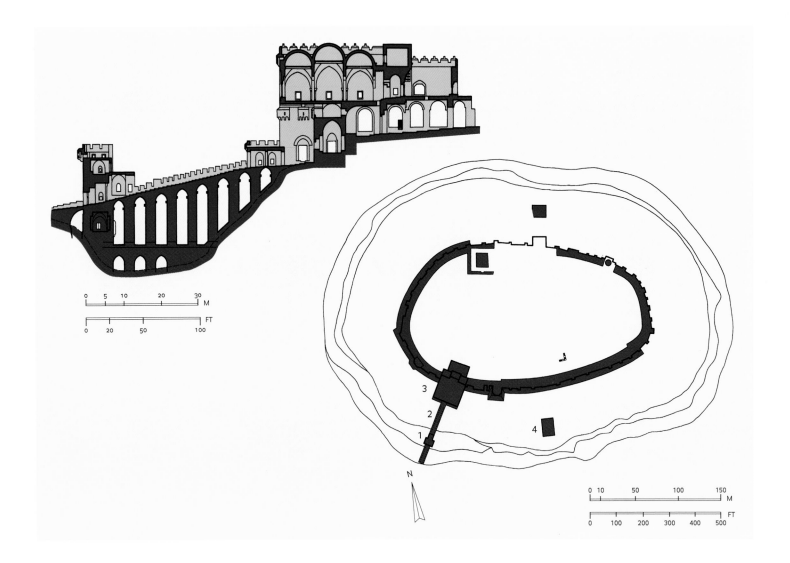

term, to the enormous tower in the center of the citadel. The rectilinear, inclined roadway was surveyed by six lines of machicolations set halfway up the walls of this bastion, in the middle of which an enormous recess, surmounted by an impressive arch, marked the entrance to the citadel. Under the vault, which housed more lines of machicolations, the gate opened on the right – facing the shields of the assailants, for soldiers held their shields in the left hand in order to leave the right hand free for combat.

This formula of the entrance way angled to the right, designed to weaken the defense of the enemy, had already been used in the Crusader's castle in Syria. It also prevented the use of a battering-ram to break down the doors. Behind the door and guarded by an iron portcullis with a cleverly forged shield, the forces which had succeeded in overcoming these first obstacles would have been confronted with a completely covered entry corridor with five bends, which climbed the escarpments leading to the upper level of the fortress. This sole route, which was completely dominated by loopholes and accessible by a series of gates, contributed to the citadel's impregnability.

The Madrasa al-Firdaus of Aleppo

When Saladin put an end to the anti-caliphate in Cairo in 1171, founding an empire in Syria, Egypt, and Arabia as far as Yemen, this constituted a triumphant return to Sunnism, after its eclipse brought about by the Fatimid sultans. If the Seljuks were defenders of orthodoxy, the Ayyubids also demonstrated a remarkable zeal for the spread of the Sunni doctrine, devoting their efforts to the creation of numerous Koranic schools.

Aleppo: an impregnable site
Lateral elevation of the barbican and of the entrance to the citadel of Aleppo, linked by an inclined bridge; and a plan of the fortified acropolis marked by forty-two towers and surrounded by a glacis smoothed by hand:
1. Barbican
2. Inclined bridge
3. Principal bastion with machicolations
4. Projecting casemate

Page 209
Advances in the art of withstanding sieges
Linking the barbican to the citadel gate of Aleppo is an inclined bridge, supported by two arches. This channeled the assailants, who could then be fired upon from the machicolations. Saladin's son completed this construction in 1209; it has been restored many times.

A magnificent acropolis
Overall view of the citadel of
Aleppo and its glacis: a crown of
towers punctuates the walls which
top the natural cone levelled by
cohorts of prisoners. In the fore-
ground is a powerful outer casemate, added in the fifteenth
century, allowing the defenders
to shoot at their assailants from
behind.

Irrigation systems
The city of Hama on the River Orontes has put the river to good use, to provide an original method of irrigation. Arab engineers built enormous wooden water-wheels, driven by the current and fitted with scoops. These fed aqueducts more than ten meters high, which then took water out into the countryside. This technique was in use before the thirteenth century, according to an Arab miniature of the *History of Bayad and Riyad*, a manuscript preserved in the Vatican Library.

Originating in Seljuk Persia, the *madrasa* made use of two forms typical of Persian architecture: the *iwan* – a large covered area with a mainly open façade – usually constructed at the edge of a courtyard; and stalactite decorations, or *muqarnas*, covering vaults and cupolas. The stalactites were ornamental motifs bordering cornices, lending emphasis to friezes, decorating capitals and springers, etc. In Persia, *iwans* and *muqarnas* were characteristic not only of mosques and *madrasas* but also of caravanserais, palace buildings and mausoleums.

The Madrasa al-Firdaus (or "Madrasa of Paradise") south of Aleppo, bore testimony to the Ayyubid's zeal for religious education. Built in 1223 by the widow of al-Ghazi, it was a massive rectangular edifice with tall, bare outer walls. The building had a symmetrical plan, 57 meters long and 45 meters wide. It was made entirely of large, even blocks of limestone in regular rows. A lateral gate, topped with a vault of stalactites carved in stone, led to an angled corridor, which in turn gave on to the central courtyard (22 meters square). In the middle there was a beautiful fountain for ritual ablutions. On three sides, a portico with arcades of pointed arches was supported by columns whose capitals were decorated with *muqarnas*. On the fourth side – to the north – was a large, square *iwan*, reached through a wide arch, 9 meters across, with large arch stones. This is where the Koran was taught. Behind the lateral porticoes were two long study halls with rows of cupolas. The third side, to the south, had an identical space, but oblong, and was used as a place of prayer. This small mosque had a superb *mihrab* in the center of the *qibla* wall, faced with colored marble with geometric motifs and intertwined arches. At the southern corners of the building were two small, square rooms, roofed with domes which had pendentives decorated with stalactites.

Advances of the *madrasa*

The arrival of the Seljuks and the consequent impetus to Sunnism produced a new type of architecture: the *madrasa* or Koranic school. The Madrasa al-Firdaus (the "Madrasa of Paradise") in Aleppo, dating from 1223, shows an austere exterior which belies the building's organization inside.

Seen from outside, the Madrasa al-Firdaus had eleven cupolas of the same diameter covering the two study halls, the mosque and the corner rooms.

This beautiful *madrasa* is a perfect illustration of the fusion between Persian forms – *iwans* and *muqarnas* – inspired by brick buildings, and the Syrian tradition of dressed stone dating back to the Roman and Byzantine eras. As for the theme evoked by its name – of paradise promised to the believer – this links it to the mosaics of the Great Mosque of the Umayyads in Damascus.

Baghdad's Last Abbasid Buildings

Just as Persian forms are echoed in Ayyubid Syria, so too Persian influences can be seen in the last buildings of the caliphs of the prestigious Abbasid dynasty – who by this time held only nominal power. Ever since the Buyid emirs had placed the caliphs under their protection, Persian influences had been felt in Baghdad. However, when the Seljuks conquered the Abbasid capital in 1055, it was as the defender of Sunnism that their leader Tughrul Beg received the title of Sultan and Sovereign of East and West. These rapidly acculturated Turks, who assimilated Persian culture during the reign of Malik Shah in Isfahan (1072–1092), succeeded in promoting Persian art, which they raised to remarkable heights.

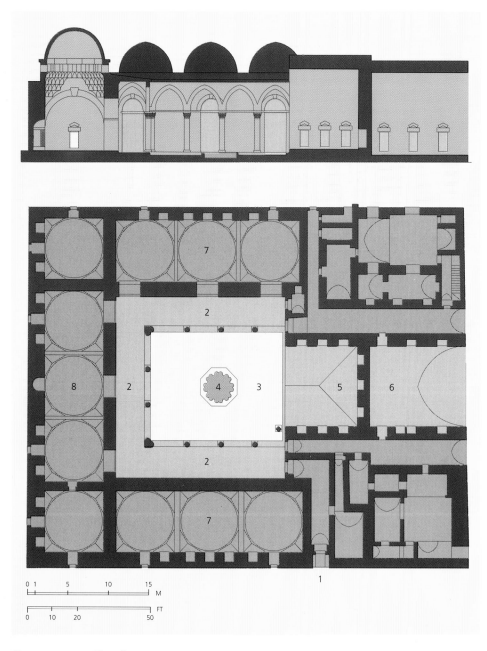

A centripetal arrangement
Longitudinal cross-section and plan of the Madrasa al-Firdaus in Aleppo. The symmetrical, rectangular building is laid out around a central courtyard with porticoes, on to which an *iwan*, used for teaching, opens.
1. Principal entrance
2. Porticoes
3. Courtyard
4. Ablutions Pool
5. Interior *iwan*
6. Exterior *iwan*
7. Two lateral halls with a row of cupolas
8. Small, oblong mosque

Muqarnas

Detail of a capital decorated with rows of honeycomb-shaped carvings forming stalactites (*muqarnas*) in the courtyard of the Madrasa al-Firdaus in Aleppo. Beehive decoration became widespread in the thirteenth-century Islamic world.

A closed world for the study of the Koran

In front of the *iwan*, with its slightly pointed vault leading to the ablutions fountain, the porticoes of the Madrasa al-Firdaus surround a paved courtyard decorated with geometric motifs.

A superb *mihrab*
The little mosque in the Madrasa al-Firdaus, Aleppo, has a superb *mihrab* that shows a coherent and disciplined design. Around the semidome at the top of the niche, polychrome marble facing with elegant, interlaced motifs, plays on the sharp contrasts in color.

Innovative formulas
Above the entrance of the Madrasa al-Firdaus are stalactite decorations carved in stone – requiring remarkable stone-cutting skill – covering the blind vault under which runs an inscription.

Spatial harmony
The rooms in the Madrasa al-Firdaus with rows of cupolas are an innovation, showing the originality of the building, which dates from the first half of the thirteenth century.

Development of Stalactites

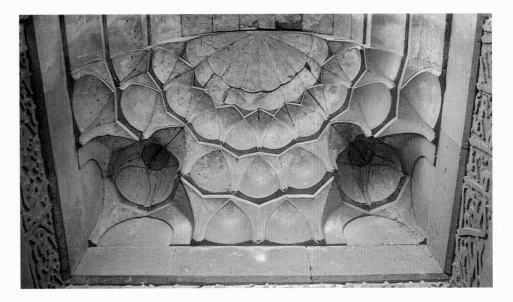

Beehives analyzed
Stalactites decorate the entrance to the Madrasa al-Firdaus in Aleppo. Their composition reveals a clever use of 16- and 32-sided polygons (plan below). The *muqarnas* continued to develop in Islamic art from the thirteenth century onwards.

The technique called stalactites, or *muqarnas*, was probably perfected by the Persians, though there is an embryonic precedent in the palace of Harun al-Rashid in Rakka, dating from the end of the tenth century. Originally in brick, the *muqarnas* were found in the Qarawiyin of Fez (Morocco) in a stuccoed cupola, dating from 1135, where they were purely ornamental above the *mihrab*. They were also present, but in brick form, in the Almoravid Qubbat Barudiyin in Marrakesh, dating from 1120.

However, in the Muristan al-Nuri, in Damascus, dating from the mid-twelfth century, we find stalactites in ashlar, attesting to an extraordinary virtuosity in the art of stonecutting. The same is true of the Madrasa al-Firdaus of Aleppo, dating from 1223. From then on, stalactites became one of the most widespread features of Islamic architecture. They are found in present-day Iran and Iraq, and in Spain and Morocco, constructed in brick, while in Turkey, Cairo and India they are in stone.

Stalactites, which result from dividing up pendentives and the resulting niches, in the form of scallopped triangles, covered *iwans*, cupolas, arches, and, in smaller form, could be transformed into ubiquitous decorative motifs. They appeared on capitals and in vaulted halls, where they formed large pendentives at the corners of domes. They were widespread, appearing in the most diverse materials and in infinitely varying dimensions, and were a distinctive characteristic of medieval Muslim art.

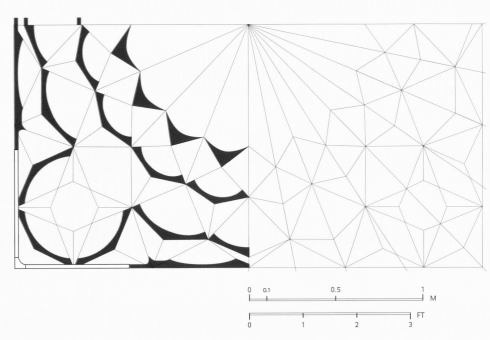

The Zubayda mausoleum in Baghdad

The high point of stuccoed brick stalactites appears in the tower-tomb of Zubayda, built near Baghdad at the end of the twelfth century by Caliph al-Nasir. Inside, the cupola with many openings shows different levels of beehive niches, based on a 32-point star.

Sugar loaf cupola

Seen from outside, the octagonal structure of the so-called Zubayda mausoleum, near Baghdad, is surmounted by a strange conical roof consisting of nine layers of salient spherical shells. The funerary monument stands amid other graves in an ordinary cemetery.

From this time onwards, Persian architects everywhere spread the idea of the *madrasa*, a building for training theologians and jurists. They also disseminated decorative systems based on stalactites, and imposed a brick architecture that they had adopted to enable their work to withstand earthquakes which occured frequently on such upland plateaus.

A century later, thanks to the weakness of the Seljuks at the time of al-Nasir al-Din Allah (1180–1225), the caliphate briefly regained its creative momentum. Al-Nasir erected buildings in Baghdad in the Persian spirit, representing a sort of swan song for the "Lesser Abbasids", whose reigns marked the end of the dynasty. The last of their line, al-Mustasim (1242–1258), was soon to perish at the hands of the Mongols who executed him mercilessly.

One interesting example of Persian influence in Baghdad is the cupola with a *muqarna* in the curious Zubayda mausoleum, constructed by the Caliph al-Nasir in memory of Harun al-Rashid's wife. This tomb was inspired by that of Imam Dur in Samarra, which dated from 1085. Nevertheless, the high cupola of the Zubayda mausoleum with nine tiers of stalactites did not stand on a square base, like its model, but on an octagon. The work undoubtedly represented a remarkable technical accomplishment, with its successive honeycomb niches which, halfway up, formed a 32-sided star. Above the star, a serried array of honeycomb niches, carved with small lunettes (like those in the halls of the *hamam*), lent a mysterious atmosphere to interior area.

Al-Nasir's successor, Caliph al-Mustansir (1226–1242), built the *madrasa* called the Mustansiriya in Baghdad. It was an oblong building (about 100 meters wide by 50 meters deep) made of brick throughout, and with a large courtyard (63 meters by 28 meters) with double axial symmetry, emphasized by four *iwans* arranged in pairs facing each other around a central pool for ablutions. One of these *iwans* was just beyond the large entrance gate, like a Persian *pishtak*. Two others, on the narrow sides of the courtyard, had wide, pointed arches framed (and much enhanced) by majestic cornices. The fourth, facing the entrance, was in the form of an oblong hall with three entrances, acting as a *haram*, or place of prayer where there was a *mihrab*.

Arcades surrounded the courtyard on two levels, behind which were the cells of the teachers and their pupils. There were about sixty rooms delineated by beautiful arches whose tympanums were decorated with subtle geometrical tracery, made by using a kind of brick mosaic with star shapes and recurrent linear patterns. These arches were typically Persian, having a central plan with four focal points, including two slightly protruding buttresses and two steeper rampant arches. Everything in this very carefully decorated brick building conjured up Persian art.

The same was true of the Qala or Palace of the Abbasids, constructed either by al-Nasir or al-Zahir before the middle of the thirteenth century. This palace has been remarkably well restored, allowing the observer to understand the original appearance of the brick building, with its central courtyard and two axial *iwans* facing each other. It was surrounded by a gallery, which led to narrow rooms. Close scrutiny of the building's plan clearly shows that, despite its rather grand name, this was a *madrasa* not a palace. Like the Mustansiriya, this school (measuring about 42 meters by 60 meters) had two levels of arcades, behind which were rooms for the teachers and students. This type of plan was of Persian origin, being organized around a central courtyard in centripetal fashion so that, like the mosques with their surrounding porticoes, the back of the building faced the street while its façades faced the courtyard. Decoration was thus concentrated in the courtyard rather than on the exterior of the building.

The distinctive ornamental feature of this building (which has many links with the Mustansiriya) lay in its lower gallery, which was covered with stalactites,

Role of the axial *iwans*
Centered around the large niches of the *iwans*, which are emphasized by their tall, decorative frames, the two stories of cells in Baghdad's Mustansiriya Madrasa are reflected in the pool used for ritual washing.

The *madrasa* with courtyard
The widthwise plan of the
Mustansiriya Madrasa in Baghdad
reveals Persian influences in its
central courtyard and ablutions
pool. The whole area is dominated
by the rectangle with two axes
which bisect the four *iwans*, each
occupying the middle of the
courtyard façade.

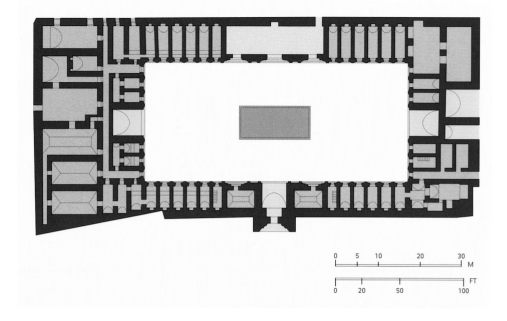

Forms of expression in brick
Both the *iwans* and the ornamental panels decorating the courtyard façade of the Mustansiriya Madrasa illustrate the high development of brick decoration, which reached its apogee towards the end of the caliphate in Baghdad. Indeed, the political decline of the Abbasids was accompanied by a marked esthetic revival under Persian influence.

Decorative glories

Muslim builders gave their imagination free rein in ornamental brick openwork, with endlessly varied motifs covering the façades of Baghdad's Mustansiriya Madrasa. Based on the octagon, hexagon or star, these designs relied on a profound knowledge of geometric structures. The creators found infinite numbers of abstract motifs to enliven the building's surfaces.

whose beehive niches and concave triangles formed petrified cascades behind the arches with their torus moldings. This very original formula reveals the more general application of a system which had previously been reserved for the most sacred elements of buildings (*mihrab, iwan*) or for load-bearing structures (corbelled galleries on minarets).

This art, which flourished in Baghdad with the last of the Abbasids, reveals not only the vigor of the Persian influence, but also the prolific creativity of a style which developed before the middle of the thirteenth century. It held the promise of a future which Arab architecture was to experience after the fall of the Abbasids, with the masterpieces created by the Mamluks of Cairo (1250–1517), the Marinids of Morocco (1248-1465) and the Nasrids of Granada (1237–1492), creators of the magnificent Alhambra Palace.

Bridge over the River Tigris
On the outskirts of Baghdad, this Abbasid bridge is an interesting remnant of the capital of the caliphs. Between two large arches, the openings in the spandrel between the spans, and the band of writing along the top of the parapet, are all that can be seen above the sand which has buried the thirteenth-century construction.

A fortified city gate

The Bab al-Wastani in Baghdad can only be reached by a bridge across the moat of the city. The sides of the roadway are protected by a parapet walk with two levels of loopholes: one level is covered, located behind a series of pointed arches; the other runs along a row of merlons whose loopholes have directional openings.

An effective defensive system

Baghdad's Bab al-Wastani gate dates from the first half of the thirteenth century. It is a vestige of the city walls built by the Abbasids during the century before the Mongol invasion. This construction is in the form of a circular bastion with an octagonal courtyard surrounded by a moat, spanned by is a bridge.

The Abbasid Palace in Baghdad
This grand name is given to what is really a lovely brick *madrasa*, with two levels of arcades, dating from the beginning of the thirteenth century. The central courtyard has a beautiful axial *iwan* and a marble basin.

The Qala

This *madrasa*, known as the "Palace of the Abbasids", has arcades edged with torus moldings (tori) which emphasize the pointed arches. The tympanums on top of the bays are decorated with intertwining designs in relief and the niches are covered with large, honeycomb stalactites evenly superimposed in groups of five. The system of *muqarnas* developed logically from the semi-dome covering the main *iwan* (opposite).

Conclusion

New Concepts of Space

This survey of six centuries of Arab Muslim architecture has shown that the Koran gave an entire people an irresistible dynamism leading to the establishment of vast empires – Umayyad and Abbasid – which changed the face of the world. Though at first Islamic art, with its remarkable masterpieces, reflected its Byzantine and Persian antecedents, it affirmed its own character from earliest days, by way of the hypostyle spaces of mosques. It was in mosques that believers gathered, adopting, for ritual prayer, a "topological" lateral arrangement which gave rise to the oblong and horizontal hall.

Islamic secular architecture continued the legacy of Roman and Sassanid palaces, dictated by complex palace ceremonies, which the sovereigns enriched with numerous technical innovations. In the Umayyad era, the center from which the caliph exercised power revived the imperial might of the Late Roman Empire, with its courtyards and its *aula regia*; while the formulas essential to the plans of the large Abbasid palaces of Samarra are akin to those of Ctesiphon under the Persian King of Kings. But the extensive scale of the establishments of the Muslim rulers, which were designed as walled cities, introduced the rectangular plan of the symbolic *chahr bagh* gardens of Persia into Arab forms of expression.

In the West, decoration during the first centuries of Islam was largely derived from the forms and techniques of Constantinople: mosaics with gold backgrounds, colored marble veneers, bronzes, etc. Agreements between caliphs and emperors prompted the development of a close artistic collaboration, which produced outstanding works.

From the eleventh century, the influence of certain Persian features spread their designs and decorative motifs over the whole of the Islamic world. This was true of the *madrasa*, the Koranic school whose concept derived from the Persian mosque, as well as of its characteristic element, the *iwan*, which was almost entirely open to the courtyard. Similarly, the stalactites, or *muqarnas*, were originally structural elements which gradually evolved into decorative ones. These honeycomb constructions were the "leitmotif" of Muslim art, just as the horseshoe arch had become a distinctive feature.

Though the Koran did not specifically forbid the use of figurative images, the respect for the second of the Ten Commandments – generally observed in religious buildings – encouraged the development of abstract geometric ornamentation. Muslim artists were intrigued by geometry and recurrent patterns, showing extraordinary imagination in the design of paved floors, marble decoration, carved stucco and especially in the decoration of the *mihrab*. Cupolas were often expressive of highly developed technical and decorative virtuosity, with plays on star-shaped patterns with 4, 5, 6, 8, 12, and 16 points, which the artisans were able to work together with rare mastery.

All these specific characteristics of Islamic art continued to develop in the Arab world after the fall of the Abbasid caliphate in the thirteenth century. They also flourished in the creative achievements of Persia, Turkey and India. This was

Flourishing *muqarnas*
Built in 1258 in the hypostyle hall of the Great Mosque of Cordoba, the Capilla Real, or Royal Chapel, is contemporary with the fall of Baghdad to the Mongols. It was built in the Mudejar style by Moorish artists for Alphonse X. This creation summarizes the technical and esthetic advances of Islamic architecture by the middle of the thirteenth century – typified by intersecting scalloped arches and delicate stalactite motifs which cover the surface of the vaulted ceiling with their honeycomb shapes.

indeed a specifically Islamic architectural language, born at the time of the Umayyads and the Abbasids over an immense area stretching from the shores of the Atlantic to the Persian Gulf. It created new spaces, specific methods and an original ornamental system which made the classical age of Islamic art a time of profound renewal where esthetic forms were concerned.

CHRONOLOGICAL TABLE

The Dome of the Rock, in Jerusalem, commemorates the "Night Journey" of the Prophet

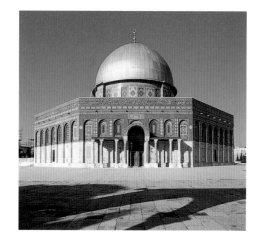

The Kaaba, in Mecca, spiritual hub of the Islamic world

2nd century B.C.

Temple of Huqqa, southern Arabia: building with a courtyard and an oblong prayer hall

3rd century A.D.

Second synagogue of Dura-Europos: pulpit and Torah-niche foreshadow the *minbar* and the *mihrab*

Monuments

After 622	Place of Prayer in Muhammad's house in Medina; *qibla* oriented towards Jerusalem
630	Orientation of the *qibla* in Muhammad's house towards the Kaaba in Mecca

638	First mosque in Kufa
642	Founding of Fustat by General Amr ibn al-As
670	Reconstruction of the mosque in Kufa
687–692	Dome of the Rock in Jerusalem

From the Beginnings to 632

632–700

From the Caliphs in Medina to the Umayyads

Historical Events

570	Birth of Muhammad in Mecca
591	Khosrau II, King of the Sassanids
595	Muhammad marries for the first time
610	Heraclius in Constantinople Muhammad hears the call to "recite"
614	Jerusalem conquered by the Sassanids
622	Emigration of Muhammad and his followers to Yathrib, which becomes Medina (Medinat al-Nabi) – beginning of the Islamic era, the *hegira*
624	Break with Judaism
626	Constantinople besieged by the Sassanids, the Slavs and the Avars
627	Heraclius takes Ctesiphon
629	Pilgrimage of Muhammad to Mecca
632	Death of Muhammad in Medina

632–634	Abu Bakr succeeds Muhammad
634–644	Omar, caliph in Medina
634	Beginning of Arab expansion: conquest of Palestine and Syria
635	The Arabs cross the Euphrates
636	Heraclius defeated on the Yarmuk
640	Invasion of Egypt
641	Capture of Nineveh and Armenia
642	Persia is attacked
644–656	Othman becomes caliph
644	Persia is subdued
647	Capture of Tripolitania
656	Othman assassinated, Ali named caliph
660	Muawiya, caliph in Damascus: the Umayyads
661	Ali assassinated
670	Annexation of Tunisia
671	The Oxus is crossed
673–678	Siege of Constantinople
680–683	Caliphate of Yazid I in Damascus
680	al-Husayn assassinated in Kerbela
683–693	Anti-caliphate in Mecca
685–705	Abd al-Malik, caliph in Damascus
693	The Kaaba is burned; the anti-caliph is put to death

The muezzin calling the faithful to prayer at the Kaaba (*Siya al-Nebi*)

The courtyard of the Great Mosque
of the Umayyads in Damascus

Portico in the courtyard of the
mosque in the palace of Ukhaidir

785 Mosque of Cordoba: construction
begun under Abd al-Rahman
832–848 First enlargement under Abd al-
Rahman II
929–961 Second enlargement: *mihrab*,
ribbed cupola, intersecting
arcades, mosaics
936–961 The palace-city of Madinat al-Zahra
c. 950 Fortress of Gormaz (Soria)
961–976 Third enlargement of the mosque
of Cordoba under al-Hakam II
987 Last enlargement of the mosque of
Cordoba under al-Mansur
999 Mosque of Bib Mardun in Toledo

706 Decision to build the Great Mosque
of the Umayyads in Damascus
707 Al-Aksa Mosque in Jerusalem
Great Mosque in Damascus
Great Mosque of Medina
710 Kasr Kharana castle
711 Qusayr Amra castle
714–715 The city of Anjar
c. 730 Mshatta castle
c. 735 Khirbat al-Mafjar castle

750 Kufa, provisional capital
762 The "Round City" of Baghdad
778 Princely Abbasid palace of Ukhaidir
836 Samarra, the new capital
Jausaq al-Kharqani Palace
848 Great Mosque of Samarra
850 Bulkawara Palace in Samarra
859–861 Abu Dulaf mosque in Samarra
862 Qubba al-Sulaybiya Mausoleum
in Samarra: first Islamic tomb
883 (892) Abandonment of Samarra as capital

700–750
The Umayyads (Continuation)

755–1031
The Umayyads of al-Andalus

750–945
The Great Abbasids

705–715 Al-Walid, caliph in Damascus
714 Submission of Spain
724–743 Hisham, caliph
744 Yazid III, caliph
744–750 Marwan II, Caliph
Alid insurrections in Khurasan
750 Defeat of Marwan II: end of the
Umayyad caliphate in Damascus

The columned prayer hall in the Great
Mosque of Damascus

711 Berbers and Arabs in Spain
712 Capture of Toledo
714 Spain subjugated: Abd al-Aziz
governor
755–788 Abd al-Rahman I, Umayyad emir in
Cordoba
788–796 Hisham, emir in Cordoba
796–822 Al-Hakam, emir in Cordoba
822–852 Abd al-Rahman II, emir in Cordoba
912–961 Abd al-Rahman III: proclaims himself caliph of al-Andalus in Cordoba
in 929
961–976 Al-Hakam II, caliph in Cordoba
976–1009 Hisham II, caliph in Cordoba
Crumbling of Arab power in Spain
1031 End of the caliphate of Cordoba

750–945 Dynasty of the Great Abbasids
750–754 Al-Saffah, caliph in Kufa
751 The Arabs defeat the Chinese
at Talas
754–775 Al-Mansur, caliph in Baghdad
786–809 Harun al-Rashid, caliph in Baghdad
800 *De facto* emancipation of Ifriqiya
813–833 Al-Mamun caliph
813–817 Caliph al-Mamun takes up residence in Merv
830 Khurasan of the Tahirids proclaims
its independence
833–842 Al-Mutasim, caliph in Samarra
847–861 Al-Mutawakkil, caliph in Samarra
868 Ibn Tulun governs an independent
Egypt
870–892 Al-Mutamid, caliph in Samarra,
and later Baghdad
908–932 Al-Muktadir, caliph in Baghdad
From 945 The caliphs under the tutelage
of the Buyid emirs

The hypostyle hall with 600
columns in the mosque of Cordoba

642, 711, 750, 791
  Different phases of construction
  of the Amr Mosque in Fustat
 827 The Amr Mosque attains its final
   dimensions
 861 Nilometer of Roda
876–879 Ibn Tulun Mosque in Fustat
 969 Founding of Cairo (al-Qahira)
   by the Fatimids
990–1013 Al-Hakim Mosque in Cairo
1030–1050 Fatimid Mausoleums of Aswan
1087–1091 Walls and gates of Cairo built
   by Badr al-Gamali
 1125 Al-Aqmar Mosque in Cairo
 1160 Al-Salih Talai Mosque in Cairo
1176–1184 Saladin provides Cairo with a
   citadel

Bartizan guarding the entrance to
the citadel of Aleppo

1089 Minaret of the Great Mosque
  in Aleppo
1154 Muristan al-Nuri in Damascus
End of twelfth century–1209
  Citadel of Aleppo
1206 Citadel of Damascus
1223 Madrasa al-Firdaus in Aleppo

Defensive system around the
courtyard of the mosque in Susah

 796 Ribat of Monastir
End of eighth century, 821
  Ribat of Susah
836, 862, 875
  Different phases of construction
  of the Great Mosque of Kairouan
 851 Mosque of Susah
 860 Aghlabid tanks in Kairouan
  Norman Sicily:
1160 San Cataldo in Palermo
1185 Ziza Palace in Palermo

800–1250
Tulunid and Fatimid Egypt

1078–1258
Seljuk and Ayyubid Syria

632–1200
Ifriqiya and Sicily

---

 868 Ahmad ibn Tulun in Egypt
868–905 Tulunid dynasty in Egypt
 905 Baghdad reconquers Egypt
953–975 Al-Muizz, Fatimid caliph
 969 The Fatimids in Egypt
 970 The Fatimids in Damascus
 973 Cairo, capital of the Fatimid caliphs
975–996 Al-Aziz, Fatimid caliph in Cairo
996–1021 Al-Hakim, Fatimid caliph
 1009 Destruction of the Holy Sepulcher
1021–1036 Al-Zahir, Fatimid caliph
1036–1094 Al-Mustansir, Fatimid caliph
1171–1193 Saladin, sultan of Egypt and Syria
1171–1250 Ayyubid dynasty

The al-Azhar Mosque in Cairo,
founded by the Fatimids

1078 The Seljuks in Damascus
1079 The Seljuks in Jerusalem
1099 The Crusaders take Jerusalem
1169–1250 The Ayyubids in Syria and Egypt
1171 Saladin (Salah al-Din), sultan
1187 Crusaders defeated at Hattin
1191 Capture of St John of Acre by
  the Crusaders
1196 Malik al-Adil retakes Jerusalem
1204 Jerusalem in Arab hands
1229–1244 Treaty of Jaffa: Jerusalem returned
  to Frederick II

 647 Arab horsemen reach Ifriqiya
  (Tunisia)
 670 Annexation of Ifriqiya, the city of
  Kairouan founded
 682 Arab defeat at Biskra
 698 Expedition against Carthage
 702 Defeat of al-Kahina and end of
  Berber resistance
 745 The Kharijites in Kairouan
 800 Aghlabid Ifriqiya becomes semi-
  independent of the Abbasids in
  Baghdad
800–812 Ibrahim ibn al-Aghlab
817–838 Ziyadatallah I
 827 The Aghlabids conquer Sicily
909–934 Al-Mahdi (Ubaidallah) spreads
  the Fatimid doctrine (Shiism)
 910 Arrival of the Fatimid caliphs
  in Ifriqiya
953–975 Caliph Al-Muizz leaves Kairouan
  and establishes himself in Egypt
  (972–973)

Courtyard of the Madrasa al-Firdaus
in Aleppo

Reception room with pool in the Aljaferiya Palace in Saragossa

Brick decoration of the Madrasa Mustansiriya in Baghdad

857, 912, 933 Qarawiyin Mosque in Fez
1070 Marrakesh founded by the Almoravids
1120 Qubba Barudiyin in Marrakesh
1135 The Qarawiyin Mosque of Fez rebuilt
1147 Marrakesh destroyed by the Almohads
1147–1157 Kutubiyya Mosque of Marrakesh
1150 Rabat founded, capital of the Almohads
1153 Great Mosque of Tinmal
1195 Hassan Mosque in Rabat (never completed)

1031–1091 "Bañuelos" of Granada
1046–1081 Aljaferiya Palace of Saragossa
c. 1050 Alcazaba of Malaga
1075–1085 Synagogue, called Santa Maria la Blanca, in Toledo
1157 Pavilions of the Alcazaba
c. 1200 Twelve-sided Tower of Gold of Seville, built by the Almohads
1258 Capilla Real of Cordoba, Mudejar construction with stalactites

1185 Zubayda Mausoleum in Baghdad
1226 Mustansiriya Madrasa in Baghdad
1228 Abbasid bridge over the Tigris, near Baghdad
1230 Abbasid Palace in Baghdad

800–1258
Almoravid and Almohad Maghreb

1031–1258
Almoravid and Almohad Spain

932–1258
The last Abbasids in Baghdad

1036–1147 Almoravid Dynasty
1061–1106 Yusuf ibn Tashufin, sovereign in Marrakesh
1086 The Almoravids in Andalusia
1107–1143 Ali ibn Yusuf
1121–1128 Muhammad ibn Tumart al-Mahdi, founder of the Almohad doctrine
1128–1163 Abd al-Mumin, Almohad caliph
1143–1147 Tashufin ibn Ali, last of the Almoravids
1163–1184 Abu Yakub Yusuf, Almohad caliph
1184–1199 Abu Yakub Yakub al-Mansur
1269 Marrakesh conquered by the Merinids

1031–1091 The "Reyes de Taifas"
1046–1081 Ahmad ibn Suleiman al-Muktadir, in Saragossa
1070–1146 The Almoravids in Spain
1147 The Almohads invade Spain Conquest of al-Andalus by the Almohads
1184–1199 Abu Yaqub Yusuf proclaimed caliph in Seville
1181–1213 Abu Abdallah Muhammad conquers the Balearics
1212 Abu Abdallah Muhammad defeated at the battle of Navasin Tolosa

945–1055 The Buyid emirs put the caliph under tutelage
946–974 al-Mutil, caliph
1055 The Seljuks take Baghdad
1094–1118 al-Mustazhir, caliph
1180–1225 al-Nasir al-Din Allah, caliph
1226–1242 al-Mustansir, caliph
1242–1258 al-Mutasim, last Abbasid caliph; the Mongols execute the caliph

Cupola with stalactites in the Qubba Barudiyin in Marrakesh

Mausoleum of Zubayda in Baghdad, with cupola

GLOSSARY

Abbasids. Second dynasty of the caliphs of Islam who, in 750, succeeded the Umayyads of Damascus. After briefly settling in Kufa, they founded their capital in Baghdad, then in Samarra, and later returned to Baghdad. The execution of the last Abbasid caliph by the Mongols in 1258 put an end to a brilliant period of Muslim power. A distinction is made between the Great Abbasids, who reigned until the middle of the tenth century, and their successors who had merely nominal authority.

Ablaq. Decorative system based on alternating black and white or dark and light layers of stones or arch stones.

Ablutions. At the five daily prayer times prescribed by the Koran, ablutions are part of the ritual purification which must precede participation in contemplation and the act of prostration and prayer.

Abraham. Venerated in the Torah and the Bible as the Jewish patriarch, he is considered the ancestor of the Jewish and Arab peoples through his sons Isaac and Ishmael. For Muslims, he is "God's friend" and is supposed to have founded the Kaaba in Mecca. He is also venerated on Mount Moriah, the Temple Mount, in Jerusalem, where God intervened as he was preparing to sacrifice his son.

Abu Bakr. Father-in-law of the Prophet, and the first caliph after the death of Muhammad. He reigned from 632 to 634.

Aghlabids. Arab dynasty in North Africa (Ifriqiya), whose governors were semi-independent of Baghdad. They reigned from 800 to 909 in Tunisia, Sicily and Malta. Kairouan at that time was a vibrant capital.

Alfiz. Rectangular frame, slightly in relief, surrounding a horseshoe arch in an Islamic building (or one influenced by Muslim art).

Ali. Cousin of Muhammad, and husband of Fatima, Muhammad's daughter. He became the fourth caliph, but the rivalry with Muawiya, governor of Syria, ended in a schism between Sunni and Shiite Muslims. Muawiya founded the Umayyad dynasty of Damascus. Ali was assassinated in Kufa in 661.

Alids. The descendants of Ali and Fatima, the Prophet's daughter, and al-Husayn, the second son of Ali. Later, Ali's followers formed the Shiite branch of Islam, asserting claims to the succession promised to the Prophet's descendants.

Almohads. From the Arabic al-muwahhidun, "partisan of Unity", according to the doctrine of Muhammad ibn Tumart who proclaimed the oneness of God. The Almohads, a Berber dynasty which succeeded the Almoravids, reigned in the Maghreb and Spain between 1130 and 1269, with their capital in Marrakesh.

Almoravids. From the Arabic al-morabitun, "brotherhood of warrior-monks". Dynasty of Berbers from the Sahara, founded by Yusuf ibn Tashufin, who reigned from 1061 to 1106 in Morocco and the Maghreb, and later in Andalusia, after 1086. They preached a strict respect for Koranic rules.

Alveole. Element of the so-called "honeycomb" structures forming stalactites. They were derived from the subdivision of pendentives into spherical triangles, corbelled one above the other. Alveoles gradually lost their structural character to become purely decorative.

Andalus, al-. The Arabic name was applied to all of Muslim Spain and was derived from "Vandalusie" or the country of the Vandals. The name persisted after the departure of the tribe of barbarian invaders, who had occupied the country before crossing into North Africa in 429.

Arcade. Architectural element composed of arches resting on a series of pillars, piers or columns. An arcade may form a portico.

Astrolabe. Instrument which provided a flat representation of the skies, used to determine astronomical data (such as the altitude of the stars or the hours) and also as a navigational aid. It also provided astrological information for drawing up horoscopes.

Atabeg. Title from the Turkish meaning a Muslim dignitary, first applied to a prince's tutor and later to a military leader holding power, as in Damascus or Aleppo.

Aula regia. Throne room or audience chamber.

Ayyubids. Independent dynasty founded by the Kurdish leader, Salah al-Din, or Saladin. The Ayyubids held power from 1171 to 1260 in Syria, Upper Mesopotamia, Egypt, Yemen and the holy cities of Mecca and Medina.

Basileus. Plural basileis. Royal or imperial title before Alexander, and later used by Byzantine sovereigns from 630 onward.

Bay. Transversal spatial unit in a covered space. The bay contrasts with the nave which is longitudinal. In a hypostyle space, the bay corresponds to the division between two rows of columns set perpendicular to the axis of the entrance.

Buyids. Dynasty of Shiite emirs who occupied Baghdad in the tenth and eleventh centuries, and who kept the Abbasid caliphs under tutelage.

Caliph. Head of the Islamic community in the line of the Prophet's successors, the caliph was the Commander of the Believers. The ceremonies at the caliph's court were inspired by Byzantine and Sassanid courtly ritual.

Call to prayer. Five times a day the muezzin calls Muslims to their ritual prayer, as prescribed by Muhammad. The first muezzin, when the Prophet was alive, was an African named Bilal. The call was made from the top of a minaret when these towers became common in Islamic architecture.

Cardo. The main street generally oriented north-south in the Roman camp.

Castrum. Roman military camp, generally square or rectangular in layout.

Chahr bagh. Persian term meaning "four gardens". The chahr bagh was a garden surrounded by walls, divided by four water channels representing the four rivers of paradise. It was a symbolic representation of the Garden of Eden.

Ciborium. A small building in the form of a canopy supported by columns.

Circumambulation. Religious practice consisting of walking around a sacred place as a sign of veneration and piety. Islamic circumambulation is practiced around the Kaaba in Mecca, the Rock of Mount Moriah in Jerusalem, and in many mausoleums and shrines where the sages of Islam are revered.

Claustrum. Finely-carved or molded panel made of brick or wood openwork, filling an architectural space while letting in light.

Cul-de-four. Roof in the form of a semidome above a niche or at the corners of a cupola resting on pendentives.

Decumanus. One of the two axes of the Roman camp (see cardo), running east-west.

Divan. Persian term initially designating the official registers, later the administrative offices of the state, and finally the sovereign's council of state. There was a distinction between the Divan i-Am, or chamber for public audiences with the prince which was part of the throne room, and the Divan i-Khas, or private audience room, used during courtly ceremonies. The formula of the two courtyards existed even before the Hellenistic kings; it developed further under the Romans and Sassanids, evolving into many forms of Arab courtyards.

Emir. Arabic title (amir) for a military commander, later a governor of a province.

Fatima. Daughter of the Prophet Muhammad who married Ali and was the mother of al-Husayn. She is especially venerated by the Shiites.

Fatimids. Ismaili Shiite dynasty of independent sovereigns who seized power in Ifriqiya in 909 and later in Egypt, in 969, where they reigned until 1171. During the Fatimid period, Muslim art, literature and science flourished.

Figurative art. The widespread ban on representational painting, and even more so on figurative sculpture, in Islam does not stem from the Koran but rather from a strict observance of the second of the Ten Commandments. It applies essentially to religious works and monuments, while secular architecture allows exceptions to this rule. The rejection of figurative art allowed the Muslims to explore complex geometrical systems (fretwork, star-shaped motifs, arabesques, etc.).

Firdaus, al-. See paradeisos.

Ghassanids. Pre-Islamic dynasty of princes from southern Arabia who ruled in the Syrian desert in the third century A.D. They were vassals of Byzantium and adopted Monophysite Christianity. Their capital was Bosra.

Hamam. Public or private baths, following the model of Roman baths.

Haram. Consecrated space in a mosque where rituals and prayer take place. It is essentially the prayer hall, but the *haram* can also include an entire sacred area, as for instance, the Temple Mount on Mount Moriah surrounding the Dome of the Rock in Jerusalem.

Hegira. "Expatriation" of Muhammad, who left Mecca for Yathrib, which became Medina (Medinat al-Nabi), the city of the Prophet. This event took place in 622, marking the birth of the Islamic era.

Horseshoe arch. An upper stilted arch with the stonework between the imports and the springing line resembling stilts.

Husayn, al-. Son of Ali and Fatima, who was assassinated in 680 in Kerbala, and is venerated by the Shiites.

Hypostyle. A hall or other large space with a roof supported by columns or pillars, forming multiple naves and bays.

Ifriqiya. Arabic word (from the Latin "Africa") designating the territories of North Africa corresponding to present day Tunisia. Its capital was Kairouan.

Imam. Arabic term meaning the leader ritual prayer (literally: "he who stands in front"). For the Shiites, the *imam* is the head of the religious community, the heir to the Islamic tradition and the interpreter of the teachings of the Prophet.

Impost. In an arcade, the slightly protruding block of stone which supports the springer of the arch.

Intrados. The curved inner surface of an arch or vault.

Ismaili. Member of the Shiite branch called "the Seveners" because they recognized seven *imams*, the last being Ismail, as opposed to "the Twelvers" who recognized twelve. For both groups, the last *imam* would be the hidden *imam*, who would reappear at the end of time after his period of "occultation". The Ismaili school gave rise to the Fatimid movement of North Africa and Egypt.

Iwan. Vaulted architectural space whose façade is mostly open (usually opening towards a courtyard). Originating in Iran during the Sassanid era, the *iwan* is a characteristic element of Islamic art influenced by Persia.

Jabal. Arabic word meaning mountain or mountain range.

Jami, al-. Arabic term meaning "he who gathers", applied to the great mosque or congregational mosque, also called the Friday Mosque.

Jerusalem. Holy city for Jews, Christians and Muslims, called "al-Quds" in Arabic. The third Islamic holy place, the Dome of the Rock is located here. It is said that the Prophet left his footprint on this rock when, astride his mount, Buraq, he made his "Night Voyage" to Allah in heaven. This is also where the venerable al-Aksa Mosque is located.

Jihad. Arabic term meaning holy war. The caliph, as the Commander of the Believers, waged a holy war against non-Muslims or "deviant" Muslims. The *jihad* is conceived of in the Koran as a collective obligation.

Kaaba. Sacred center of Islam in Mecca where the Black Stone is venerated in the sanctuary supposedly founded by Abraham. It is the object of the pilgrimage instituted by the Koran which every practicing Muslim must carry out at least once in his life.

Kasr. Arabic word for a fortified castle or palace in the desert.

Kharijite. Name given to the followers of Ali who rallied to Caliph Muawiya and formed a strict egalitarian sect.

Kibla. See *qibla*.

Koran. Literally "the recitation", the sacred book of Islam. It is a collection of the teachings of Muhammad. The revelations of the Prophet were written down in the form of fourteen suras, or chapters, of uneven length, about fifty years after his death. His teachings were completed by the *hadiths*, or conversations of the Prophet, transmitted orally and written down in the eleventh century. They form the *sunna*, that is the tradition which allows clarification of the Law.

Kubba. See *qubba*.

Kufic. Early form of Arabic alphabet which is stylized and rectangular, supposedly originating in Kufa. It is a monumental script,

appearing at the beginning of the eighth century in lapidary inscriptions; it was also used in the classical period (ninth and tenth centuries) for copying the sacred text of the Koran.

Lakhmids. Fourth century A.D. dynasty of pre-Islamic Arab princes in Iraq, vassals of the Sassanids. Their capital, Hira, was near the future Kufa.

Limes. Defensive fortified line on the frontier of the Roman Empire.

Madrasa. Koranic school whose architectural form follows the tradition of mosques, with Persian-style courtyards containing *iwans*. The *madrasa* was extensively developed during the era of the Seljuks — recently-converted Turks who spread the *madrasa* as a means of re-establishing orthodox Sunnism when Islam had, in large measure, gone over to the Shiite camp.

Mahdi, al-. In Shiite eschatology, the hidden *imam* who would reappear at the end of time.

Maqsura. Enclosure around the most sacred area of the mosque (the *minbar* and *mihrab*) where the sovereign attended prayers. By extension, it also came to describe the pierced screen-like slabs or panels (*claustra*) surrounding a tomb.

Martyrium. See shrine.

Maydan. Large, open space or plaza, with many uses: army parades and victory marches took place here; it also served as a hippodrome or polo field.

Mihrab. Niche in the *qibla* wall, above which was a vault with a "cul-de-four" or a small internal space preceded by an arch, forming the mosque's holy of holies. The *mihrab* indicates the direction of Mecca, towards which the worshipper faces when performing the ritual prostrations of Islamic prayer.

Minaret. Tower from the top of which the muezzin calls Muslims to prayer.

Minbar. Raised seat or pulpit placed to the right of the *mihrab* in mosques. From the top of the steps of the *minbar* the preacher addresses the congregation.

Miraj. See Night Voyage.

Muezzin. The official in a mosque whose duty is to call the faithful to prayer, by chanting his call from the top of the minaret. According to tradition, the first muezzin was a companion of

Muhammad, an African named Bilal.

Multifoil arch. A decorative arch formed by a succession of small concave segments, or scallops.

Muqarnas. Ornamental stalactites which adorns the cupolas or corbels of a building. The original structural function of these honeycomb-shaped decorations became secondary to their decorative aspect. They are characteristic of Islamic architecture. See also Alveoles.

Nabataeans. Pre-Islamic Arab tribe which settled in the Petra region of present-day Jordan in the first centuries A.D., from where it controlled trade between India and the Hellenistic, and later the Roman, world. The Nabataean language was a script providing a transition from the Aramaic to the Arabic alphabet.

Nave. Longitudinal area in a covered building, as opposed to the bay which is a transverse subdivision. Naves are often formed by arcades perpendicular to the *qibla*.

Night Voyage. Vision in which the Prophet was transported "spiritually" from Mecca to the "distant mosque" of Jerusalem, and then raised to heaven in order to contemplate the divine image. It is mentioned in a very allusive way in sura XVII, 1 of the Koran — a mysterious text which has given rise to a profusion of theological commentaries.

Omayyads. See Umayyads.

Paradeisos. Greek term of Persian origin (*pairidaeza*) which the Arabs translated as *al-firdaus*, used to describe the Garden of Eden and the abode of the blessed in the other world.

Pendentive. The concave spherical triangles or sprandels in an area covered by a dome, which form the link between the square plan and the circle of the dome. Not to be confused with the squinch.

Peribolus. Consecrated area surrounding a church or temple delimited by an enclosure or wall.

Pilgrimage. Obligation of all believers of Islam to go at least once in their lifetime to the holy places of Medina and Mecca in order to perform a complex ritual, culminating in the circumambulation of the Black Stone of the Kaaba.

Pishtaq. Persian term which is used to designate a large rectangular screen framing an Islamic *iwan* or gateway (to a mosque, *madrasa* or mausoleum).

Portico. Structure composed of load-bearing elements – pillars and columns – which support a façade or the interior of a roofed area. The portico may have either architraves or arches; if the latter, it is called an arcade.

Prayer. Ritual contemplation to which believers are called. The Koran prescribed five daily prayers accompanied by recitations, gestures and prostrations.

Proskynesis. Part of courtly ceremonies during which one prostrated oneself before the deified sovereign. Proskynesis was an essential part of court ritual for the Islamic caliphs who inherited the custom from the Persian kings and from the Greeks and Romans.

Qasr. See Kasr.

Qibla. Wall of the mosque oriented perpendicularly to the direction of Mecca, in which the *mihrab* is placed. During prayer, the faithful prostrate themselves towards the *qibla*.

Qubba. Originally meaning a domed building, it has come to mean an Islamic mausoleum or tomb.

Ribat. Monastic fort, often established in the frontier areas of Islam.

Sassanids. Persian dynasty, reigning from 224 to 651 over an empire that stretched from Mesopotamia to the River Indus. It was a power with which the Romans of the Late Empire, and later the Byzantines, clashed. Though the dynasty collapsed before the assault of the Arab forces of Islam, its cultural traditions were largely taken over by the Abbasid caliphs.

Seljuks. Dynasty of sultans of Turkish origin who were Sunnis. They ruled Persia and Mesopotamia in the eleventh and twelfth centuries. The first Seljuk sultan was Tughrul Beg (1038–1064). In 1055, the Seljuks took Baghdad, and in 1071 they defeated the Byzantines at the battle of Manzikert, spreading into Anatolia. After having taken Damascus in 1078 and Jerusalem in 1079, their leader founded the Sultanate of Rum. They experienced setbacks during the Crusades, later re-establishing themselves in the thirteenth century, only to be defeated by the Mongols in 1243.

Shiites. Muslims who follow the tradition represented by Ali, the husband of the Prophet's daughter, Fatima. For them, the heir to the authority of the caliphate should be a direct descendant of Muhammad. Shiites differ from the orthodox Sunnis in the importance given to the role of the caliph.

Shrine. Christian sanctuary dedicated to a martyr. Architecturally speaking, the *martyrium* usually had a central plan with a cupola.

Spandrel. Triangular space between the side of an arch and ist rectilinear frame; also applied to the area between two arches in an arcade, and the area of a vault between adjacent ribs. This area is often decorated, especially around the *mihrab*.

Squinch. Small arch or vault placed diagonally across an interior corner.

Stalactites. See *muqarnas*.

Sunna. Religious theory and practice governing the lives of Sunni Muslims, an ethic based on the Muhammad's messages, found either in the Koran or in the *hadiths*, forming the Tradition.

Sunnis. Followers of orthodox Islam based on the Sunna who recognize the four first caliphs of Medina as heads of the Muslim community, followed later by the Umayyads and the Abbasids.

Temenos. Greek term meaning a sacred space or precint; an urban area consecrated to a deity.

Tesserae. Small marble, glass or semi-precious cubes used to create a mosaic.

Tie rod. Wooden or metal strut connecting the imposts of an arcade to ensure stability and to brace an architectural structure.

Tiraz. Arabic word for a state-owned textile workshop, which produced the precious cloth, adorned with gold thread, used for courtly robes.

Trefoil arch. A triple arch having three concave sections.

Triconch, or Triple apse. Space having a trefoiled shape with three lobes, one axial and the other two to right and left. This spatial plan appeared in numerous edifices of the late Roman Empire and became a characteristic of the formal audience chambers in the palaces used for court ritual in Byzantium.

Tulunids. Dynasty founded by Ahmad ibn Tulun, governor of Egypt, who declared independence from the Abbasids and seized power in Fustat in 868 A.D. The Tulunids reigned in the Nile valley until 905.

Twelver Shiites. Branch of Shiism which venerated the twelve *imams* who handed down the interpretation and the doctrine of the Islamic Law. The twelfth *imam* was in a state of "occultation", that is, he had disappeared, and his return as *mahdi* would come at the end of time, according to Shiite eschatological belief.

Umayyads. Islamic Arab dynasty of Damascus which succeeded the first caliphs of Medina. Founded by Muawiya in 660, it was heavily influenced by the Byzantines. It ended in 750 with the assassination of all the family members – except one, who founded a dynasty in the far western reaches of the empire, in recently-conquered Spain.

Yathrib. Original name of the city where Muhammad, accompanied by his followers, took refuge after his "expatriation" (the *hegira*), marking the birth of the Islamic era (622). The city was soon to be named Medina.

Zirids. Independent dynasty which ruled from 972 to 1152 in Ifriqiya. The Zirids revolted against the Fatimids of Cairo and recognized the Abbasid caliphate in 1041. But the Alid caliphs took their revenge by sending the barbarian tribe of plunderers, the Beni Hilal, who laid Ifriqiya waste.

Ziyada. Outer courtyard surrounding a mosque, separating it from its urban surroundings.

BIBLIOGRAPHY

GENERAL

Atasoy, N., A. Bahnassi, M. Rogers: *The Art of Islam*, Paris, 1990.

Bamate, H.: *Apports des Musulmans à la civilisation*, Geneva, 1962.

Cahen, C.: *L'Islam des origines au début de l'Empire ottoman,* in: Histoire universelle/14, Paris, 1970.

Grabar, O. and D. Hill: *Islamic Architecture and Its Decoration A.D. 800–1500, A Photographic Study*, London, 1964.

Encyclopaedia of Islam, 9 vols., Leiden, 1960.

Ettinghausen, R. and O. Grabar: *The Art and Architecture of Islam, 650–1250,* New York, 1987.

Hoag, J. D.: *Islamic Architecture*, New York, 1977.

Jazari, Ismail ibn al-Razzaz: *The Book of Knowledge of Ingenious Mechanical Devices,* Translated from the Arabic and annotated by D. R. Hill, Dordrecht/Boston, 1974.

Koran, Translated with notes by N. J. Dawood, London and New York, 1990.

Papadopoulo, A.: *Islam and Muslim Art*, New York, 1979.

Renz, A.: *Geschichte und Stätten des Islam, von Spanien bis Indien*, Munich, 1977.

Sourdel, D. and J. Sourdel-Thomine: *La civilisation de l'Islam classique*, Paris, 1968.

Stierlin, H.: *Architecture de l'Islam, de l'Atlantique au Gange*, Fribourg, 1979.

Stierlin, H.: *L'Architecture islamique*, Que Sais-Je?, Paris, 1993.

Vogt-Göknil, U.: *Mosquées, grands courants de l'architecture islamique*, Paris, 1975.

Voyageurs arabes, Translated into French by P. Charles-Dominique, Paris, La Pléiade, 1995.

ORIGINS

Alföldi, A.: *Die Ausgestaltung des monarchischen Zeremoniells am römischen Kaiserhofe*, in: Mitteilungen des Deutschen Archäologischen Instituts, Römische Abteilung, 50, 1935.

Aufstieg und Niedergang der Römischen Welt (ANRW), collected essays, Berlin 1975–1978.

Constantine VII Porphyrogenitus: *Le Livre des Cérémonies*, Text by A. Vogt, 4 vols., Paris, 1935.

Gaudefroy-Demombynes, M.: *Mahomet*, Paris, 1957.

Goodenough, E. R.: *Jewish Symbols in the Graeco-Roman Period*, Vol. 9, 10, 11, Symbolism in the Dura Synagogue, Bollingen Series, XXXVII, New York, 1964.

Herzfeld, E.: *Der Thron des Khosro*, in: Jahrbuch der Preussischen Kunstsammlungen, 41, Berlin, 1920.

Kraeling, C. H.: *The Synagogue: Excavations at Dura Europos*, Final Report VIII, Part I, New Haven, 1956.

Lambert, E.: *La Synagogue de Doura Europos et les origines de la mosquée*, in: Semitica, III, 1950.

L'Orange, H. P.: *Studies on the Iconography of Cosmic Kingship in the Ancient World*, Oslo, 1953.

Pirenne, J.: *Arabie préislamique*, in: Encylopédie de la Pléiade, Histoire de l'Art, Le Monde non-chrétien, Paris, 1961.

Rathjens, C. and H. von Wissmann: *Vorislamische Altertümer*, Hamburg, 1932.

Smith, E. B.: *Architectural Symbolism of Imperial Rome and the Middle Ages*, Princeton, 1956.

Smith, E. B.: *The Dome, A Study of the History of Ideas*, Princeton, 1960.

Stierlin, H.: *Cités du Désert, Pétra, Palmyre, Hatra*, Paris, 1987.

Stratos, A. N.: *Studies in Seventh-Century Byzantine Political History*, London, 1971.

Stratos, A. N.: *Byzance au VIIe siècle*, Volume I: *L'empéreur Héraclius et l'expansion arabe*, Volume II: *Les premiers Héraclides et la lutte contre les Arabes*, Lausanne, 1980.

UMAYYADS AND ABBASIDS

Bell, G. M. L.: *Palace and Mosque at Ukhaidir, A Study in Early Mohammedan Architecture*, London, 1911.

Crespi, G.: *L'Europe musulmane*, La Pierre-qui-Vire, 1982.

Creswell, K. A. C.: *Early Muslim Architecture*, 2 vols., Oxford, 1932–1940 (2nd edition of vol. I in 2 parts, Oxford, 1969, reprint NY, 1980).

Creswell, K. A. C.: *A Short Account of Early Muslim Architecture*, London, 1958 (revised and enlarged, Aldershot, 1989).

Duncan, A.: *The Noble Sanctuary*, London, 1972.

Ecochard, M.: *Filiation des monuments grecs, byzantins et islamiques*, Paris, 1977.

Gabrieli, F. et al.: *Le Califat de Bagdad, La Civilisation Abbasside*, Lausanne, 1988.

Golvin, L.: *Essai sur l'architecture religieuse musulmane*, 3 vols., Paris, 1974–1978.

Herzfeld, E.: *Geschichte der Stadt Samarra*, Hamburg, 1943.

Sauvaget, J.: *Châteaux omeyyades de Syrie*, in: Revue des Etudes islamiques, XXXIX, 1967.

Sauvaget, J.: *La mosquée omeyyade de Médine*, Paris, 1947.

Syrie, Mémoire et civilisation, Catalogue IMA, Paris, 1993.

EGYPT

Brandenburg, D.: *Islamische Baukunst in Ägypten*, Berlin, 1966.

Canard, M.: *Le cérémonial fatimide et le cérémonial byzantin*, in: Byzantion, No. 21, 1951.

Creswell, K. A. C.: *The Muslim Architecture of Egypt*, 2 vols., Oxford, 1952–1960.

Hautecœur, L. and G. Wiet: *Les Mosquées du Caire*, Paris, 1932.

Raymond, A.: *Le Caire*, Paris, 1993.

Volkoff, O. V.: *1000 Jahre Kairo, Die Geschichte einer verzaubernden Stadt*, Mainz, 1984.

SPAIN AND THE MAGHREB

Al-Andalus, Las Artes islamicas en España, Catalogue MET, Madrid, 1992.

Aziz, Ph.: *La Civilisation hispano-mauresque*, Geneva, 1977.

Glick, T. F.: *Islamic and Christian Spain in the Early Middle Ages*, Princeton, 1979.

Golvin, L. and D. Hill: *Islamic Architecture in North Africa, A Photographic Survey*, London, 1976.

Lévi-Provençal, E.: *La Civilisation arabe en Espagne*, Cairo, 1938.

Lézine, A.: *Architecture de l'Ifriqiya, Recherches sur les monuments aghlabides*, Paris, 1966.

Marçais, G.: *L'Architecture musulmane d'Occident*, Paris, 1954.

Sanchez Albornoz, C.: *L'Espagne musulmane*, Translation of Arabic texts by C. Faraggi, Paris, 1985.

Staacke, U.: *La Ziza: un palazzo normanno a Palermo: La cultura musulmana negli edifici dei Re*, Palermo, 1991.

Stierlin, H.: *L'Essor de l'Espagne*, Paris, 1990.

Terrasse, H.: *La Mosquée Al-Qaraouiyin à Fès*, Paris, 1968.

Torres-Balbas, L.: *La mezquita de Córdoba y las ruinas de Medinat al-Zahra*, Madrid, 1952.

Index – Monuments

ACKNOWLEDGEMENTS AND CREDITS

For the photographs not taken by Anne and Henri Stierlin, Benedikt Taschen Verlag wishes to thank:

Pages 94/95: © Drawing Francesco Corni/*Bell'Europa* n. 15, 7/94.

Page 9: © Abdelaziz Frikha, Tunis.

Pages 24, 35, 126, 132, 133 (right): © Georg Gerster, Zumikon.

Page 195: © Chris Lignon/ONA Foundation, Casablanca.

Pages 189, 190 (top, right), 191, 192, 193: © Roland & Sabrina Michaud/Rapho, Paris.

Page 46: © Mohammad al-Roumi, Damascus.

The engravings of Louis Mayer, dating from 1802, which appear on pages 138, 143 (top), 159 and 206, and the architectural summaries on pages 99 and 110 (right) are taken from the *Essay on Architecture of the Arabs and Moors in Spain, Sicily and Barbary,* by Girault de Prangey, 1841. They were photographed with the kind permission of the head of the University and Cantonal Library, Dorigny, Lausanne.

We extend our special thanks to Alberto Berengo Gardin for preparing the plans on pages: 18/19, 26, 28, 29, 30, 34, 39, 50, 59, 66, 71, 74, 77, 78, 81, 96, 98, 106, 118, 119, 127, 130, 132, 135, 142, 144, 153, 163, 174, 178, 183, 188, 193, 196, 198, 208, 214, 218, 221.